Copyright © 2020 by Chr rights reserved under all ....ions. No part of this publication may be reproduced, distributed, or transmitted in any form or by any means, including photocopying, recording, or other electronic or mechanical methods, without the prior written permission of the author, except in the case of brief quotations embodied in critical reviews and certain other noncommercial uses permitted by copyright law.

ISBN 978-1-7348337-0-6

LIFE180 Media
Attn: CareerNext Agency
1801 W Azalea Dr
Chandler, AZ 85248

The scanning, uploading, and distribution of this book via the Internet or via any other means without the permission of the publisher is illegal and punishable by law. Please purchase only authorized electronic editions and do not participate in or encourage electronic piracy of copyrightable materials. Your support of the author's rights is appreciated.

For ordering information or special discounts for bulk purchases, please contact CareerNext Agency.

Versions of this content, along with interviews and additional insights can be heard on the Executive Job Search Secrets Podcast, visit https://apple.co/2JH82v7

EXECUTIVE JOB SEARCH SECRETS

CHRIS KIRKPATRICK
& MATT BAECHLE

CONTENTS

	FORWARD	10
	DEDICATIONS	15
	INTRODUCTION	18
01	**THE FUNDAMENTALS OF TODAY'S EXECUTIVE SEARCH**	**28**

- **The Playing Field** — 23
- **Why High Performers Need To Modernize Their Job Search** — 34
  - #1: Anywhere from 70% to 90% of senior level positions are never advertised. Instead, they are part of the "hidden" job market. — 38
  - #2: Technology has made it more difficult for your résumé to get past computerized "gatekeepers" so you will even be considered for a position. — 40
  - #3: More than ever, who you know (and/or who you are connected with) will determine whether you hear about a particular job. — 42
    - Stage One: "Who Do I Know?" — 43
    - Stage Two: "Who Do They Know?" — 44
    - Stage Three: "Where Can I Go to Find Good Candidates?" — 44
- **You Must Change Your Mindset Around Job Hunting** — 46
- **Why Executive Job Searches Fail - and How to Set Yourself Up For Success** — 48

02 MYTHS AND PITFALLS THAT WILL KEEP YOU FROM FINDING THE POSITION YOU WANT — 52

- Job Search Myth #1: You Need To Have a Résumé. — 55
- Job Search Myth #2: If I am the right fit, I will get through the Applicant Tracking System (ATS) — 57
- Job Search Myth #3: You Need to Speak to the HR Department. — 58
- Four Pitfalls to Avoid on your Search — 60
  - Pitfall #1. You're doing what everyone else is doing. — 60
  - Pitfall #2: You feel uncomfortable in the role of job seeker. — 61
  - Pitfall #3: You have no system for success. — 63
  - Pitfall #4: You find yourself on a downward spiral, out of control. — 67
- The Solution? Become Your Own Recruiter — 68

03 THE PSYCHOLOGY FOR A SUCCESSFUL SEARCH — 72

- #1: The Sooner You Stop Looking for a Job, the Sooner You'll Find One — 74
- #2: You're In Control of Your Results — 75

04 THE GAME PLAN FOR YOUR SUCCESSFUL EXECUTIVE JOB SEARCH — 78

- Take Control of Your Search — 78
- STEP 1: Seek Clarity — 81
  - Get Your Mind Right — 84
  - Areas To Seek Clarity — 86
    - What Are Your Passions And Interests? — 87

Copyright © 2020 | Executive Job Search Secrets

- What Are Your Goals — 88
- How Do Company Values Align With Yours? — 89
- Company Culture — 90
- How Does Company Size Play Into Your Decision? — 91
- Do You Have Any Geographic Constraints? — 92
- Industry Verticals — 95

- **STEP 2: Personal Branding & Packaging** — 96
  - **Your Passion Statement** — 97
  - **Make Your Dream Big Enough to Make You Uncomfortable** — 102
  - **Required Documents For A Successful Branding Campaign** — 103
    - Resume — 104
    - Cover Letter — 105
    - Thank You Letter — 106
    - Executive Proforma — 107
    - Optimized LinkedIn Profile — 108
  - **Your Brand — Know What You Are Selling** — 110
  - **What Is Your Brand?** — 111
  - **Questions to Ask Yourself as You Are Developing Your Brand** — 113
    - What are you selling? — 113
    - Who are you? — 114
    - What sets you apart? — 115
  - **Begin A Personal Branding Campaign** — 117
  - **Use Social Media (Especially LinkedIn) to Build Your Brand** — 120
  - **Basic Principles For Internet and Social Media Success** — 123
    - Be Searchable — 123
    - Be Laser Focused — 124
    - Be Seen as an Expert in Your Field — 124
    - Be Consistent — 125

CONTENTS

- Be Patient ... 126
- **Choose Your Platform** ... 126
- **LinkedIn** ... 127
  - Free or Premium LinkedIn Subscription? ... 128
  - LinkedIn Sales Navigator ... 129
  - Networking on LinkedIn ... 130
  - How To Get People To Engage With Your Profile On LinkedIn ... 131
- **Adam Johnson** ... 134
- **Building Your Brand on LinkedIn** ... 136
  - Be Known ... 137
  - Be Liked ... 138
  - Be Trusted ... 139
  - Be Hired ... 140
- **Using LinkedIn to Look for Work When You're Still Employed** ... 141
- **Make the Most of LinkedIn's Social Selling Index** ... 142
- **Twitter** ... 145
- **Facebook** ... 146
- **Personal Website, Blogs and Online Media** ... 147
- **STEP 3: Identify and Target Ideal Companies & People** ... 150
  - The Cold Market ... 152
  - Your Search Begins with Your Network ... 157
  - How To Discover Opportunity and Connect with Key Decision Makers ... 162
- **STEP 4: Connecting and Cultivating Relationships with Key Decision Makers** ... 165
  - Network Your Way to Decision Makers by Developing Relationships with Influencers in Your Field ... 166
  - Find the Decision Makers by Starting at the Top of Your Targeted Companies ... 168
  - The Pros and Cons of Different Modes Of Communication to Reach Decision Makers ... 170
    - Email ... 171
    - Phone Call ... 173

04 continued

- Sending a Letter — 175
- Social Media — 177
- Face to Face — 178
- **THE 3 P's x 2: Package, Position, Promote and Prepare, Be Proactive, Persist** — 181
  - Prepare — 183
  - Be Proactive — 184
  - Persist — 185
- **Communicating with an Executive Recruiter** — 186
  - Don't be overly friendly — 186
  - Don't expect career coaching — 187
  - Don't ask for insider information — 188
  - Don't request special treatment — 189
- **Three Reasons Why a Recruiter or Network Contact is Not Calling You Back** — 190
  - Mistake #1: You made it all about you — 190
  - Mistake #2: No accountability or call to action — 191
  - Mistake #3: You appear needy or as if you're selling something — 192
- **Go For No** — 194

05 HOW TO NAVIGATE THE INTERVIEW — 199

- **The Confidence/Competence Loop** — 200
- **We All Make Decisions Emotionally** — 202
- **How to Prepare for the Interview Using our EPIC™ System** — 203
  - Level 1: The face of the company — 204
  - Level 2: Just under the surface — 206
  - Level 3: Market landscape — 209
  - Level 4: In the trenches — 210
  - Level 5: The core — 211

CONTENTS

- Before the Interview: Your Appearance Checklist — 212
- Great Questions Invite Revelation — 215
- How to Answer the Question "What's Your Greatest Weakness?" — 218
  - How to Formulate an Answer for Any "Weakness" Question — 220
  - Additional Key Questions You'll Should Be Prepared To Answer — 222
- The Last Thing to Ask in the Interview — 237
- Handling the Offer and Negotiation Stage — 240
- How To Receive And Handle The Offer — 241
- Negotiating The Best Possible Offer — 242
- Having a Job Custom Created — 244
- Work with CareerNext — 250

Testimonials & Reviews

"Chris and Matt pack so much information, insight and application into these pages. They've developed a modern proactive strategy to executive-level job finding. It's easy to see why the executives who work with them end up landing their ideal position 4x faster than people who apply more traditional job search methods."

Robert Hotchkin, International Minister, speaker, 5-time author and media host

"Navigating the job market is very complex and overwhelming once you start making over $100k per year. We use Chris and all of the information he shares in Executive Job Search Secrets as the foundation of helping veterans secure their ideal executive position when they are entering the private market."

Jim Pare, Executive Director, Veteran BizOps

"Everyone has a different interpretation of success, and this book helps you understand which questions to ask to continue moving your career toward that pinnacle of your career journey. It truly teaches how to position yourself as a leader and exemplifies the path for your respected brand to ensure that your future prospective company can't deny your value!"

Josh Poso, CEO, Vast Computer Solutions

"Executive Job Search Secrets is the map that will allow you to market your specialized knowledge, talents, and abilities into your ideal position that not only offers great money and benefits, but also the more meaningful intangibles like greater creative contribution and lasting significance. The time for resumes, recruiters and job boards is past - this book will show you how to find opportunities that no one else will ever hear about. The process worked for me... I'm a believer, and it can work for you too if you apply what you'll learn here."

John Dallas "JD", Director of West Coast Operations, (National Restaurant Chain)

FORWARD

Why this book? Why Now?

As you read this book, know that it is written with an assumption. That you are reading it for a reason.

The US Department of labor estimates that the average executive search takes one month for every $10,000 of desired income. That means if you are making $200,000, you better plan on looking for nearly two years.

That's simply an unacceptable and unnecessary number. The average executive makes $600+ per day, so being out of work can get expensive.

Why is it that executives struggle so much at finding positions? After all, you are an executive for a reason. You are amazing at what you do, so this shouldn't be so hard….right?

The reality is that 90% or more of the jobs you are looking for are never going to be posted or advertised. Most of the jobs you are looking for are in the hidden or unpublished market. Those positions won't find *you*, you need to find them.

It's actually kind of ironic that out of the thousands of executives that our team speaks with every year, every single one of them knows that as soon as you become reactive in business, you are in trouble. However, when it comes to searching for a job, virtually every single one of them is implementing a reactive search approach.

Sure it feels fairly proactive because they put time into their resume, submitting it online, and sharing it with their professional contacts. They reach out to their network and have the classic conversation around, "hey Joe, I just wanted to let you know that I am in the market. I was wondering if I could share my resume with you that way if you see anything or hear of anything you could keep me in mind and pass my info along?"

Other people go to recruiters or headhunters with a sense of excitement. They don't realize that recruiters and headhunters represent the company and their best interest, not yours. They may be able to help you, but it's still going to be highly competitive (often times more so than normal), and their job is to help the company find the best person. Not to help you be that best person. They are looking for the square peg for their square hole. If you are not the perfect fit, you won't get the job.

Those strategies may feel proactive on the surface, but they are reactive. You are putting your search in the control of other people. Then you basically sit back and wait?

The only reason successful people would resign to that sort of approach is because they don't know any other way. This book is the other way. The way that will help you find what you are looking for 400% faster than industry average.

BY THE TIME YOU ARE FINISHED READING YOU WILL:

- *Discover and/or refine your brand, so you will be able to attract your dream role - and be positioned to land it.*
- *Stop making expensive and timely mistakes that are slowing down your search.*
- *Know the process to find the opportunities you are looking for.*
- *Know how to stop wasting time on LinkedIn and leverage it as the powerful networking tool it can be.*
- *Know how to get personal introductions to people who can advance your career.*
- *Approach your search from a position of power.*
- *Have a business plan to land your position.*
- *Have the tools and resources to execute that plan.*

We have gained a reputation for being a top Executive Career Management organization in the country for a reason. The process you are about to learn works 100% predictably - if you follow it.

A lot of things you probably think to be true about executive search will be challenged. So get ready to accelerate your job search. You control the speed in which you land your next position.

DEDICATIONS

To my wife, partner, and best friend, Hannah. I would not be able to do any of this without you. I truly believe God put us on this earth to be together.

The adventure we have been on to reach this place—working for large companies, and then starting our own, all while building our family, has been extraordinary.

It is a gift to work with you side by side in every aspect of life, every single day. Thank you for your support through the journey to get here. And thank you for your actual support in managing getting this book put together. It could not have been done without you.

To my amazing kiddos, Knightley, Kanon, and Kierland! You are the inspiration that makes me want to leave this world a better place. There is no greater joy I have than being your father.

To Matt Baechle, my co-author. Thanks for being an amazing friend and business partner and driving me to get this book DONE so we can help the world. Writing this book (3 different times in 3 different ways) was not easy and wouldn't have been done without you.

-CHRIS KIRKPATRICK

To all the executives currently going through a career transition and looking for a competitive edge, we wrote this book for you. It's always been a bucket list item for me to create something that I believe can make a significant difference in people's lives while providing the help, knowledge and encouragement we all seek from time to time.

Ironically, I got involved in this project because I needed help in making a career change and industry transition, so I just lived the experience you're starting. I learned very quickly throughout my journey what doesn't work, what's changed technology-wise, as well as what strategies and systems I needed to leverage in order to achieve success quickly.

I'd like to also acknowledge a special group of people that have been instrumental in my career and professional development and without whom I would not be the person I am today. These are the individuals I consider my personal Board of Directors: Angela Baechle (my wife and best friend), John Baechle (my father), Jim Caggiano, Scott Finger, Bill Glaser, Ken Husted, Chris Joslin, Kevin McAllister, Tim Murawski, Chris Prentice, Leo Pusateri and Chris Sells. I cannot thank you enough for your support, guidance, love and friendship over the years.

To my co-author, Chris Kirkpatrick, without your passion and determination this book would have never happened. You are an awesome friend and have been instrumental in helping me re-discover my true passion while creating this blueprint for others. I know you will continue to make a positive impact on many people's lives. Keep pursuing your dreams!

-MATT BAECHLE

INTRODUCTION

What do race cars and your job search have in common?

I have always been more into SUV's than cars. The idea of hoping into my Jeep and exploring some corner of the Southwest is one of my favorite things in life. However, there was one 3 day period in 2006 that was one of the best and most impactful 3 days of my life.

I went through the Bondurant High Performance Driving School. You probably need a little back story. To make a long story short, I was getting some personal mentorship from TV personality, Greg Behrendt.

If you were to Google Greg, you would see that he is a standup comedian and made his fame as a consultant for the show, Sex in the City, and as a daytime talk show host on

NBC.

I still remember Greg blindfolding me as I got into the car to head who knows where. They lifted my blindfold as we pulled into the racetrack. "What are we doing here?" I asked. You can imagine my laughter when he suggested with a straight face that I needed to get behind the wheel of a car to learn how to take control, develop more confidence, and build more trust in my environment.

It wasn't until about a decade later that I realized the impact those days had on my life.

The first part of the class was getting into a Corvette Z06 with over 700 horsepower with the lead instructor, Mike. The idea of getting into a virtual rocket ship on a racetrack seemed like a lot of fun. I had no idea how terrified I could become in a (fairly) controlled environment.

We harnessed in and faced a professional "road

course" with tight, blind corners, up and over bumps and dips. My knuckles turned white as the tires screamed around every corner as he pushed the car faster and faster, up to its absolute limits. I had no idea a car could go around a nearly 90 degree turn at almost 90 MPH and stay on its wheels. But my instructor did. I still remember how casual Mike looked as he smirked over at me, all while I was trying to not to hyperventilate in the passenger seat.

As Mike crossed the finish line after the second lap, he slowed the car to a stop. My heart was beating nearly out of my chest. He confidently drops, "I am going to teach you how to do that." I remember thinking, "Dude, you're insane if you think I will be able to drive like that". But I was hooked, and excited to give it all I had.

One of the first things we did was hop into the "slide" car, which is specially designed to spin out of control anytime at the instructors will - and it's the rookie driver's job to recover.

Mike explained it to me something like this: When you are driving at this level, things are going to happen that are out of your control. Someone will bump you or crash in front of you. There will be debris in the road or maybe someone will blow a hose and leave a puddle of oil or other fluids in the track that will send you sliding or spinning across the track. You never know when it is going to happen…only that it's inevitable it will happen.

Down the track we went in the slide car. He had me take different lines into the corners as I got more and more comfortable. It was like he was a Jedi and could sense when I got just a little bit too comfortable… My edge began to relax and he hit the button for the first time. Instantly the wheels started screaming as the car spun out of control careening 70 miles an hour down the track.

It was pure chaos for me. I cranked the wheel back and forth trying to get the car to straighten out, as I was now headed straight for the wall of tires on the infield. I remember him jerking my head around, instructing me to "STOP LOOKING AT THE WALL!" Although he didn't scream at all. Actually, it was quite the opposite. It was almost insane to me how calm he was.

I turned my head to look up the track. Low and behold, the

car straightened out and we came to a stop. "What did you learn?" he asked. "Ummmmm....to not look at the wall?," I said as a question - not having a clue.

"You got it!", he said. "The car is going to go wherever you are looking. Have you ever seen a car go off the road and somehow it manages to hit the only pole for half a mile? It's because they are so focused on avoiding it, they stare at the one thing they don't want to hit."

As I started down the track again, I was committed to not lose focus. I wasn't going to let him catch me by surprise this time.

Wrong! Before you knew it, I was spinning. I knew exactly what I needed to do. "Just don't look at the wall," I told myself, as I tried to focus straight where I wanted to go to straighten the car out. But I couldn't help it. It took another jolt from Mike to get my head straightened out once again.

As we came to a stop I was like, "What the heck, man! I knew what I needed to do. I thought I had it. I'm sorry."

But he was so calm and told me that nobody gets it right by the second try. I asked him, was he ever scared of spinning wildly out of control towards a wall at 70+ miles per hour?

In a synopsis, this was his response: "Never. I have done this 1,000 times. I know exactly how the car feels and what it can take. I know when the tires will grab. And if it ever gets too out of control, I have a backup control switch."

For the record, I executed the spin perfectly on my fourth try. It was a pretty proud moment.

It wasn't until around 10 years later that I would really grasp the impact of that experience.

We all have areas of our lives that we are as comfortable with as Mike is with spinning at 70+ mph.

You see, Mike had done this 1,000 times. While I was thinking I was going to die, he was calmly listening to every screech, squeel, and engine roar. He knew what was going to happen before it happened. And if it didn't go exactly right, he knew how to respond. Essentially, he had a system that he knew would produce a predictable result.

So I ask you this - What is the area (or areas) in your work and personal life that are like that for you? Where you are so comfortable, you know what is going to happen before it happens. You have done it 1,000 times. Where people you work with are astounded at your level of confidence and expertise in tough situations.

How does this happen? Because like Mike, you spent years mastering your craft.

My friends, this area of second nature confidence and control is exactly what makes you awesomely unique, and an exceptional investment opportunity for any company.

However, just because you are amazing at what you do, doesn't make you amazing at finding a job at what you do. There is a lot that you need to know, and be able to execute well in crisis, to be successful in today's highly competitive digital job market. Just as my daily commute does not qualify me to roll in Mike's lane.

The fact that you are reading this book tells me you are

interested in advancing your career. Maybe by choice, maybe by necessity. If you're reading this, it's probably fair to say you're "like Mike" at what you do.

Regardless, when it comes to creating and conducting a high-level job search, at some point you will likely feel like you're gripping the wheel of a Corvette Z06 as it spins wildly out of control at 100+ mph... towards a wall. The good news is, you don't need to feel that way. You don't have to be out of control of your results.

Bondurant Racing has developed a system to quickly teach people how to prepare for the unexpected, overcome challenges, gain confidence and achieve positive results.

So do we. CareerNext has carved a niche for ourselves by creating a proven system to help clients like you simplify your executive job search and overcome all the key challenges, so you can be much more effective and get proven results - even in the slide car.

You probably are well aware that you don't find executive level positions the way you find low level positions. In fact, as much as 90% of executive level positions are never posted, and are never advertised. Spending countless hours searching LinkedIn, Indeed, ZipRecruiter, Monster, or any other online job board in unlikely to yield success. And, this is just the start and the most obvious of potential problems you're likely to encounter.

This book is all about the secrets and the system you need to know (and execute under pressure) to find your next ideal role faster, and land it for more money, and a lifestyle you deserve.

Don't just read this book - study it. It will be the playbook for your success. The truth is, the only variable to your success is you. Keep your focus on where you want to go, and let us be your "Mike".

We are honored that you would trust us with your time and look forward to helping you achieve greatness in your life and career. Start your engines, let's do this.

THE FUNDAMENTALS OF TODAY'S EXECUTIVE SEARCH

01
The Fundamentals of Today's Executive Search

If what you thought was true about your executive job search turned out to be completely false—
when would you want to know?

THE PLAYING FIELD

One of my favorite quotes is, **"What got you here isn't going to get you where you want to go."** While that rings true throughout almost all of life, it is especially true when it comes to your executive job search.

The good news is that your ability to climb through the ranks says a lot about who you are, your value proposition, and why a company would view you as a great investment opportunity.

Think about it. Your journey to becoming an executive probably involved a lot of loyalty and dedication as you climbed the ranks in one, maybe two or more companies. You might have started at an entry-level position and risen consistently through the ranks from individual contributor to manager to Director to VP to President or other C-suite position.

But now, for whatever reason, you want (or need) to look for a new position, or a new company, or both. (Or perhaps you're smart enough to realize that in today's changing world, no one's job is safe and all of us should keep our personal brand updated and relevant.) The problem is that most executives haven't had the need to look for a position in years because they have grown inside of their current company or have been recruited by a former colleague to a new position.

Regardless, if you are reading this, my guess is you are feeling a bit lost for possibly the first time in your successful career. If you haven't looked for a leadership position in the past 5 years, things have changed dramatically when it comes to your job search.

As you know, only a very small percentage of people have what it takes to reach your level. According to the U.S. Department of Labor's Bureau of Labor Statistics (BLS), in 2017 only 5.1% of positions in the United States were considered to be management-level—and only 1.7% could be called top executives[1].

However, something happened while you were on this journey through the ranks, and you didn't even know it. As soon as you reached an income somewhere in the range of $100,000 to $150,000, the game changed. Statistics from the BLS clearly shows that if you are a senior executive, you are in the top 2% and leadership positions are more challenging to attain.

---

[1] *"May 2017 National Occupational Employment and Wage Estimates, United States," Bureau of Labor Statistics, U.S. Department of Labor, https://www.bls.gov/oes/current/oes_nat.htm. Last Modified Date: 30 March 2018. Accessed 2 April 2018.*

So it's not surprising that your job search can take a very long time. According to a frequently quoted study by the U.S. Department of Labor, the average job seeker takes roughly one month for every $10,000 of desired income to find their next position. If you are an executive making anywhere from $100,000 to upwards of $200,000, that can mean you'll spend anywhere from 10 months to almost two YEARS in your job search!

What's worse, **up to 90% of executive jobs never even appear on the open market!**

The executive job search world can leave you feeling like you are stranded in a desert. You plod along slowly, looking for water. Before long, you come across an oasis with palm trees and water with shade. It is what you have been looking for—and more! Only the closer you get, the dimmer it looks. As you finally reach the oasis, you realize it's a mirage. It doesn't exist.

Executive positions can be the same way. You hear about (and sometimes see) these positions posted, but most of the time they are elusive to find. When you finally get close enough where you think you have a chance at landing the job, it vanishes, and oftentimes you have no idea what happened, or why.

Especially once you reach upwards of $150,000+, traditional job hunting no longer works in any capacity. It is a completely new playing field requiring a completely different process. If you are looking for your next executive position and you find yourself feeling lost on knowing where to start or frustrated at your lack of success, chances are that you simply don't understand the environment or playing field of the game as it is played today.

You don't find executive level positions the way you find other positions. Meaning, many of these positions are rarely posted. However, there ARE ways to "game the system" and land the position you want, at the salary you want, in a reasonable amount of time. You just need to know how to play the game the way it is played in the 21st century.

WHY HIGH PERFORMERS NEED TO MODERNIZE THEIR JOB SEARCH

Years ago, getting a new job was a pretty straightforward process:

- *You created your resume*
- *You looked in the local newspaper for positions and reached out to a bunch of recruiters*
- *You applied for all positions that fit your skill set*
- *You received one or two job offers and accepted the best opportunity*

It was that simple. But today, the job-search process is excruciating. If (like many of our clients) you have been in the same position or the same company for more than a decade, you're probably unaware that the way typical job searches are conducted has changed dramatically over the last 15+ years. And, job searches will continue to change as new technology and new industries come online.

The last time I had to interview for a job was 19 years ago in the year 2000. And, I remember clear as day what I did. I personally updated my resume and sent it off to about 5 recruiters and within a couple weeks, I had several interviews lined up.

I decided to engage and interview with two companies within med-tech industry targeting a $200k sales role and quite honestly, I went into those conversations "winging" it. I ended up receiving a great offer from one of the companies, but the company I didn't receive an offer from was the opportunity I preferred. Looking back, I'm sure that I would have benefited from some professional help and that likely could have made the difference.

At that time from a technology standpoint, LinkedIn didn't exist and dial up internet was still the standard. If I wanted to find the best companies based on my criteria, how was I going to identify them on my own? It's amazing how quickly things change with time.

Today's digital age has significantly evolved the game for both how companies seek talent and how job seekers identify the best companies. Social media has created many new avenues and opportunities for job seekers to cultivate relationships with key decision makers.

While it's true that technology has made it easier for job seekers, it's also true that it's made it more difficult to stand out. There are three critical factors that you need to know and take into account when you start a "new school" executive job search.

THEY ARE: ─────────────

Before you read further, allow me to define what I mean by the term "executive". We don't mean this just in the traditional sense of being in a "C-Suite" role. For the sake of this book, we are using the term "executive" synonymously for any position earning $100k+ since the principles for success are the same at each level.

Let's talk about each of these factors

Three critical "new school" executive job search factors

FACTOR 1

Anywhere from 70% to 90% of senior level jobs are never advertised. Instead, they are part of the "hidden" job market.

FACTOR 2

If you find an opportunity within the "open" job market, Applicant Tracking Systems (ATS) and other technology has made it more difficult for your résumé to get past computerized "gatekeepers" so you can even be considered.

FACTOR 3

More than ever, who you know (and/or are connected with) will determine whether you or not you hear about a particular job. Identifying great executive-level opportunities is all about effective networking and I believe every executive job seeker would benefit from some helpful coaching on this topic.

#1: Anywhere from 70% to 90% of senior level positions are never advertised. Instead, they are part of the "hidden" job market.

There are two different types of markets, "open" and "hidden," and it is vital to understand the difference between them.

The open market consists of all of the resources available to the public. It includes job boards, recruiters, headhunters, etc. The problem is that only 10 to 30% of executive opportunities end up on the open market. And the higher the position and salary, it's less likely the position will be advertised at all.

The hidden market is where roughly 70 to 90% of the executive opportunities are located. You reach the hidden market through your connection with influencers and decision makers, by going directly to an employer via one of the company employees, and so on.

Contemplate those statistics for just a moment. In what world or with what business would you spend 80+% of your time where only 10 to 30% of your potential exists? If you look at your search like a business opportunity, that is a recipe for going out of business, FAST. For your own sanity, when you're looking for a new executive position, you might want to avoid the open marketplace if at all possible. Why? When a position reaches the open marketplace it becomes a highly competitive environment. According to Glassdoor, every corporate job opening attracts on average 250 resumes and only 2% receive an interview.

Additionally, when recruiters or headhunters are retained to submit candidates for an open role, they oftentimes are finding 30 or more people with backgrounds similar to yours to interview for the role—not exactly what I would call ideal.

But as you can see, before any opportunity hits the open marketplace, it spends time in the hidden marketplace. Every job or opportunity has existed long before it ever hits the open market. The secret to you finding the position you are looking for, against less competition and in a shorter time frame, is knowing how to discover and market yourself to the opportunities found in the hidden market.

#2: Technology has made it more difficult for your résumé to get past computerized "gatekeepers" so you will even be considered for a position.

Suppose you do go on a job board in the open market and you spot a position at a company that you feel is a perfect fit for your skills and experience. You send over your résumé with a brilliant cover letter and wait to be called in for an interview. But you never hear anything because no one at the company ever saw your résumé. Why? It didn't contain a particular search term or keyword and the job board's screening software rejected it!

That's the world we're in today. Whenever you apply for a position via a job board or a company's HR department, your résumé is likely put through an Applicant Tracking System (ATS) that screens for particular keywords describing qualities, skills or experience the company wants. So even if you're a perfect fit for the job, without those keywords in your résumé, no human will ever see it.

Unfortunately, the ATS is not the only technology barrier you will face. Most large employers also have adopted mechanical communication protocols that reserve live contact with a human being for the very end of the recruiting pipeline.

HERE'S WHAT THE JOB APPLICATION PROCESS LOOKS LIKE:

1. *You fill out an employment questionnaire online.*
2. *If you make it past the first screen, you may be asked to take a personality profile test or an aptitude test to see if you will "fit" with the rest of the team.*
3. *Once you're past that, there will be more requests for personal information, maybe a background check, and more delays.*
4. *You'll have to go through all of this BEFORE you ever have contact with a human being either by phone or email!*

If you're irritated by this kind of treatment, consider the fact that today's HR departments are understaffed and spread paper-thin. They're expected to handle employee relations, training, compensation and benefits and recruiting for several hundred team members. It's no wonder that they try to automate as much as they can and save the human touch for the best few candidates for a position.

Technology has made it more and more challenging to reach decision makers. Luckily, there's a way to get past the technological "gatekeepers" and put your name in the hat for the position you want.

The digital age has shifted the pendulum full swing back to the side of personal contacts and relationships. The old adage, "It's not what you know, it's who you know," has never been more true than it is today.

#3: More than ever, who you know (and/or who you are connected with) will determine whether you hear about a particular job.

Filling positions with the right people is getting more expensive—and hiring mistakes are cost-prohibitive. A 2017 study by Korn Ferry Hay Group revealed, "The cost of replacing a manager within 6-12 months of their hire is 2.3 times the person's annual salary…. For a senior executive position, the replacement cost could amount to $1 million or more[2]. That cost is one of the many reasons that CEOs and HR hiring managers are relying on referrals and personal relationships rather than ads or job boards to find the best candidates.

HERE'S THE PROCESS THAT MOST DECISION MAKERS GO THROUGH WHEN THEY NEED TO FILL A JOB AT THE EXECUTIVE LEVEL.

Stage One: "Who Do I Know?"

We are all human, and humans like familiarity. It is comforting. That's why when a decision maker (CEO, owner of a company, VP or Director, etc.) decides they need to bring on new talent, the first stage a job search goes through is the "Who do I know that would be a perfect fit for this position?" stage.

---

[2] "The Talent Forecast: Move Beyond Cost Per Hire," 16 May 2017, https://www.kornferry.com/institute/the-talent-forecast-move-beyond-cost-per-hire. Accessed 2 April 2018.

If you think about it, it just makes sense. The decision maker doesn't want to take huge risks or allocate tons of resources scouring the planet for top talent. With their success and network they think they must know someone who can do the job. So they try to find someone they know and have experience with that could fill the role.

Stage Two: "Who Do They Know?"

If they don't know anyone (or are unable to convince someone they do know to make the move) the next step is to ask people in the first level of their network if they know anyone who would be a good fit for the job. After all, this is still better than hiring someone they don't know or trust.

If you have jumped through the ranks quickly, or been promoted by changing companies, I'm willing to bet you probably were personally referred into a position or "recruited" directly by the decision maker themselves through a process of networking. That's just how it works.

Stage Three: "Where Can I Go to Find Good Candidates?"

Even with referrals, finding good talent can be challenging. That's why between 5 to 10% of the time, opportunities make it through stages one and two and then onto the open marketplace: places like job boards, recruiters, headhunters, executive placement firms and so on. Companies can utilize these services to help them find quality talent. However, finding that talent is typically expensive for the company and far less certain than hiring based on a referral.

At the end of the day, when given the two options of hiring from either a recommendation or through a job board or recruiter, leadership would prefer to hire from a recommendation almost every time.

The effective way to search is to spend at least 80% of your time focused on networking, cultivating relationships and reaching out to influencers and decision makers.

There is an art and science to successful networking. For example, if you have ever reached out to anyone on LinkedIn or used your network and not gotten the response you were hoping for or expecting, there is a reason why. It can be a little more challenging to begin, but we promise that's where your fastest results will come from an overwhelming majority of the time.

The reality is, if you are looking for the most direct path to your next leadership position, you have to make sure you are taking a modern approach. Not doing so can cost you extra months of your life and tens of thousands of dollars.

YOU MUST CHANGE YOUR MINDSET AROUND JOB HUNTING

To access the hidden marketplace, get past technology barriers and conduct a successful job search, you need to get into your mind that **you are NOT job hunting: you are job sowing…or farming.**

Think about it this way, hunters are always looking for something to kill. They spend hours tracking down their prey, but if they step on a branch and spook the animal they are hunting, they have to start all over. On the other hand, job sowing is networking. It's planting seeds. It's farming. Your job is to plant seeds strategically (network) and water those seeds (follow up) until you can harvest the crop (you land a job). When you focus on sowing and networking rather than searching for a job, you are making connections with people. It's all about timing and chemistry. You need to have both. When you have the right chemistry at the right time, that's when the right opportunity unveils itself. When you make the right connections at the right time, magic happens.

Another way to look at it is to think of yourself as being on the campaign trail. Your job is to share your value proposition with as many people in influential positions as possible. That way, when a position opens up, you want to be the first person that comes to mind for them to contact for the position.

Okay...so I'm guessing all this all sounds logical. However, what's interesting based on our thousands of conversations with executive job seekers, is knowing what you should do is totally different than being able to execute on these strategies effectively. The phrase, "don't confuse simple with easy" couldn't be more spot on.

Today, we all want social proof for everything we do, whether it's a restaurant, movie, car, vacation, etc. So much of what we do revolves around recommendations of our peers. Finding your next executive position is no different. The only difference is YOU are the movie and you need to get some friends or connections to recommend it!

This small shift in mindset may seem like a small thing, but it is everything when it comes to a successful search.

WHY EXECUTIVE JOB SEARCHES FAIL
AND HOW TO SET YOURSELF UP FOR SUCCESS

Now you understand the parameters of finding a new executive position in the 21st century—but that doesn't mean you're ready to conduct a successful job search. You need to prepare, not just your résumé, but also your mind and emotions for the process of finding the executive position you want.

This may be harder than you think—especially if you're one of the many executives who have never had to find a job because the job has always seemed to find them. But if this time you are either out of work (or know you will be soon) it can be very uncomfortable to look for a job. Fears can come up. You may be embarrassed by being unemployed. If you've been looking for long enough, there may even be some desperation.

Almost every executive we've met has had some strong emotions around looking for a new position. Even if your job is secure right now and you are the one who feels that it's time to find something else, it's very likely that you feel restless, or underutilized, or unrecognized, or just plain bored. All of those emotions can get in the way and cause you to make some unproductive choices when it comes to finding the right new position.

Throughout the rest of this book you will learn the secrets of planning and executing a successful job search. But first, you need to get your mind and emotions ready for success. You see, the big picture reason that most high-level job searches fail is because executives don't recognize they are selling a multi million-dollar product.

YOU ARE A MULTI MILLION-DOLLAR PRODUCT.

In your job search you are promoting a precious commodity: your valuable human capital. If you want to have a successful executive search, you must remove emotion and create a strategic search plan that will enable you to market your valuable human capital to the people who can give you the position you want.

However, before you create your strategic plan, you need to challenge the way you think about what that plan should include. Much of what you think to be true about an executive job search is, in fact, not true at all. In the next chapter we will be exploding some persistent myths and pitfalls that may keep you from finding the position you want.

MYTHS AND PITFALLS THAT WILL KEEP YOU FROM FINDING THE POSITION YOU WANT

02

Myths and Pitfalls that Will Keep You from Finding the Position You Want

Perhaps the greatest myth of all is the idea of job stability. Since you're reading this book, we'll assume that you are either looking for a new position right now, or at least contemplating leaving your current job and finding a new one. But in today's world, there IS no real job stability. Job security is a historical legend publicized by the 40/40 Club. You remember them? The men and women who worked for the same company for 40 hours a week for 40 years and then retired with a $40 gold watch?

That's no longer even close to reality. In 2015 the Bureau of Labor Statistics published a study of the work lives of Baby Boomers born between 1957 and 1964. These Baby Boomers held an average of 11.7 jobs between the ages of 18 and 48. That means they only spent 2.5 years at any given position![3]

---

[3] "Frequently Asked Questions: Number of Jobs Held in a Lifetime," Bureau of Labor Statistics, National Longitudinal Studies, https://www.bls.gov/nls/nlsfaqs.htm#anch41. Accessed 2 April 2018.

"The "job stability" mindset is toxic to your long-term career success. If you want to remain successful and happy throughout your career, you have to acknowledge that you will never really be stable in any position."

The statistics for executives are pretty much in line with these numbers. According to a 2013 survey by Blue Steps, 55% of senior executives have already worked for two to three different organizations. And only 44% plan to stay at their current company for another two to five years. "The majority of senior-level executives are willing to make a career transition if the right opportunity came along," the survey concluded.[4]

You have to adapt an entrepreneurial mindset as an executive in today's environment. Think of yourself as a solo-preneur who is a product in the marketplace that is constantly for sale. To do this successfully, you need to be proactively managing your career and perpetually developing your brand!

---
[4] "How Long Is a Senior-Level Executive's Tenure?" Blue Steps survey, 27 Aug 2013, https://www.bluesteps.com/blog/how-long-executive-tenure-infographic.aspx. Accessed 2 April 2018.

The moment you land your next position, you should update your marketing materials (your resume, executive proforma, & LinkedIn profile). Always network, always be open to conversation. Like you would as an entrepreneur or a corporation running their business, you must always be proactively keeping your brand relevant and open for future opportunities. It's almost a certainty your current (or next) position won't be your last.

Now that we've exploded the job stability myth, let's look at three others that directly affect your job search. Everyone believes these myths to be true, but you should throw them out the window immediately.

JOB SEARCH MYTH #1: YOU NEED TO HAVE A RÉSUMÉ

Technically, that may be true: you do need a résumé. However, you need to shift your fundamental understanding on what the résumé is designed for as a tool—and more importantly, how to use that tool. How your résumé is written and formatted is important, but few people understand how to use it as a tool of landing their next executive role.

We will touch more on the proper way to use résumés as you go through the book, but for now just know that changing your belief about how to use your résumé probably will be required. And while you technically need to have a résumé, a high percentage of our clients land their executive position without using one.

The résumé tends to be a convenient way for executives to "get ready to get ready" —meaning that they think until that résumé is perfect, they can't get started. Even when the résumé is "perfect," it is a tool that is improperly used a high percentage of the time. In fact, most résumés end up accomplishing the exact opposite of the intended outcome (unless, of course, your goal is to be removed from the running for a position).

Think about it this way - resumes are perfect for submitting to job postings online or with recruiters. If we know that 70-90% of the jobs are not going to be on job boards or represented by recruiters, why would you put so much weight on its importance?

Sure, it's important. But nobody ever hired a resume. It's just like John Maxwell says, "nobody cares how much you know until they know how much you care. But once they find out how much you care, you had better know something." That last part is where your resume comes in, "once they find out how much you care, you had better know something."

Your resume should be used as a historical document to backup everything you speak to. If you are leading with your resume at the executive level, you're putting yourself at a disadvantage.

> ***Job Search Fact:*** If you want to improve your search, stop worrying so much about how to write your résumé and start thinking more about how to use it as a tool to accomplish the job.

JOB SEARCH MYTH #2: IF I AM THE RIGHT FIT, I WILL GET THROUGH THE APPLICANT TRACKING SYSTEM (ATS)

First of all, the only instances that the ATS is even relevant is for the jobs that are posted and advertised. That means for most executive level opportunities, the ATS doesn't even come into play. Yet, I see more energy and concern centered around making sure their executive resume is ATS optimized.

Even if your ideal position is found online, studies have shown that only 5 out of 1000 applications even make it through the ATS systems. That means no matter how talented, credentialed, and qualified you may think you are, the odds are stacked greatly against you.

You can see why it is absolutely vital to take a different strategic approach to any job search at the $100k+ level.

JOB SEARCH MYTH #3: YOU NEED TO SPEAK TO THE HR DEPARTMENT.

One of the most common misconceptions among most executive job seekers is the need to reach HR people. After all, they are the people who do the hiring, right? Wrong. Depending on the level of role you're targeting, you need a strategy that will help you reach key decision makers: C-suite Executives, Owners, Presidents, Board Members, Vice Presidents, Regional Directors and so on. Whether that's connecting with these people yourself, or being referred by someone they know, like and trust, your goal is to bypass HR on the front end of the conversation whenever possible—until, of course, you've already accepted a great job offer from the company.

> *Job Search Fact:* The days of using HR to land an executive position are far behind us.

We hope you're starting to understand the realities that you'll be facing as you start looking for that new position. But understanding the facts is not enough. You also must avoid four pitfalls that can sabotage your best efforts and keep you from quickly and effectively getting the job you want.

FOUR PITFALLS TO AVOID ON YOUR SEARCH

PITFALL #1

YOU'RE DOING WHAT EVERYONE ELSE IS DOING.

If you're going about your search like everyone else—looking at job boards, sending out résumés, targeting dozens of recruiters, maybe calling a few people in your personal network to let them know you're available—then you're going to end up as one of those executive job seekers the Department of Labor described as taking 10 to 20 months to find a job. There are not many people who can go that long without work mentally and emotionally, not to mention financially. And the sad part is that it doesn't need to be that way.

The problem with the traditional job search methodology as outlined above is that the approach is completely reactive. From a business strategy perspective, waiting for the phone to ring with someone saying they would like to meet or speak with you is not a productive strategy.

There is a saying, "If you want to achieve 1% results, you can't do what 99% of people are doing." This has never been truer than within executive job search space. If you want different results and a competitive advantage, you need to stop doing things the same way as everyone else (unless of course they are getting the result you want).

This book is designed to show you how to "think different," as Apple said in a famous ad. It will give you a taste of the process that CareerNext guides its clients through to help them find their ideal position 400% faster than the industry average.

Pitfall #2

YOU FEEL UNCOMFORTABLE IN THE ROLE OF JOB SEEKER.

Oftentimes executives struggle because they have never

had to look for a position before or possibly, it's been awhile. Maybe opportunities have always found them and they have never had to ask for help.

Well, there is another old saying: "Just because the ostrich buries his head in the sand doesn't mean the lion's dinner plans have changed." The reality is, if you want to find your next executive position successfully, there are certain principles that you must follow. The principles of success are absolute and clear, and you ignore them at your peril. Look, you are obviously amazing at what you do. You wouldn't have reached the level in your career you have if you weren't. However, the executive search space is an entirely different game and playing field. There is no shame in acknowledging you don't understand it fully. After all, if you want to be good at something, you better be ready to be bad at it first (or not quite as awesome as you would like to be).

Like anything else in life, getting comfortable with being uncomfortable about some of the required activities that only you can do in your search is a requirement. You can either conquer that fear or struggle for the next two years. It's your choice.

PITFALL #3

YOU HAVE NO SYSTEM FOR SUCCESS

As important as growing your necessary skills for success, having a predictable system that you can plug those skills into is equally important.

Almost every executive we speak to understands that as soon as you become reactive with any facet of your business, you are in trouble. Why would it be any different with your job search? The answer is, it's not. In the same way you build systems in business to handle whatever comes up, you need a system to make sure your job search is efficient and effective.

In fact, systems are just leverage. I once listened to a talk by a sales leader named Myron Golden. In his talk he said, "you can make up with leverage what you lack in ability." What he was talking about was leveraging systems to reach success.

You know this to be true, you see it every day. Who sells more hamburgers than any other restaurant in the world? It's McDonalds. I think we can all agree that McDonald's does not produce the best hamburgers in the world, so how is it they have sold the most? SYSTEMS!

If you don't know him, Myron suffers from side effects from having Polio as a child. He can't run - in fact, he walks with a significant limp. During his talk, he brought a very fit person from the audience on stage and asked the crowd, "if we were to race, and he was running, who would win?" Everyone said that the fit gentleman who looked like he worked out 6 days per week would win.

That's when Myron paused and said, "depends if i'm on a bike. You see, I didn't say I was running, only that he was." Click, it all made sense. The bike was leverage. It was a system that could allow a handicap person to beat a person who's fitness was far superior in a race.

The same goes for your job search. It's not the person with the most talent or the best education that gets the job. It's the person who has the best system and strategically promotes themselves to the right people and companies at the right time - that's who gets the job.

However, you have to make sure your system is relevant. If it's still stuck in the 20th century, you're in trouble. It used to be that the "best practices" way for most executives to find a new job was to write a résumé (after all, anyone with a college education can do that, right?), blast said résumé out onto the internet, connect with a couple recruiters and wait for the phone to ring. Easy, right? But that system is reactive—you're waiting for others to get back to you. And in today's job market, that's just not good enough.

Think of it this way. Name a part of your life more important than your career. God? Family? Okay, that's two. Question: How great would your relationship with your family be if you just waited for your spouse or children to ask for your attention?

You have to proactively put your time and energy into your relationships for them to work—and you can't rely on a third party to do it for you. Why would you rely on third parties for your success in something as important as your relationship with God, your family, or your career?

My guess is you are shaking your head side to side right now thinking, "No way!" Well, when you wait for someone else to contact you, that's exactly what you're doing. You can't just "phone in" your relationship with God or with your family—or with your career. You have to be proactive. You can't put your success in the hands of third party people and just wait for your phone to ring.

When it comes to your job search, you need a proven system for success that you can plug into, and then you must be 100% proactively engaged in it. You need a system that challenges you to grow and be the best version of you that you can possibly be. After all, if you are looking to find that job of all jobs, you are going to need to stand out…and this is how it starts: with the right system.

Don't jump ahead now, but later in the book, we are going to show you the 5 step system that you can leverage for success in today's job market.

PITFALL #4

YOU FIND YOURSELF ON A DOWNWARD SPIRAL, OUT OF CONTROL.

Let's assume you are following that 20th century version of a job search. You got your résumé to a stage where it is marketable and you blasted it out to job boards, recruiters, headhunters, executive search firms and so on. And then you waited.

And waited...

AND WAITED….

Here's the truth: the average executive making over $100,000 need to submit to over 200 job postings online to receive 5 responses. That's over 200 hours of work on average to get just 5 responses - and you're lucky if you get 1 or 2 screening interviews out of the process. I don't care who you are, that is going to hurt your confidence.

Once your confidence gets shaken, you are hesitant to ask for help because the fear of rejection takes over. You try to fit yourself into the mold of every opportunity that does come your way, but because it doesn't seem completely authentic, you finish second or third place for the position.

That is what leads to the downward spiral, mentally and emotionally. We have seen executives who have made over $1 million per year in their previous company struggle to land a position making $200,000 per year because of this exact situation. It is happening every day to executives all over the world. Keep reading so it doesn't happen to you.

THE SOLUTION?

BECOME YOUR OWN RECRUITER

To take control of your executive job search, you need to do what an executive recruiter is supposed to do: find positions that are a great match for your skills and experience, campaign for you to be interviewed and then help you with negotiating the offer.

But here's the truth: most executive recruiters don't represent you at all. Instead, they represent the company who pays them a finder's fee once they fill the position. A recruiter doesn't care if you land the position, or if one of the other 30-plus candidates do. As long as one of his candidates is hired, he gets paid.

The reality is that in most scenarios, you are a greater asset for any recruiter than he would or could be for you. (Oftentimes, you being in the recruiter's database is what helps him to sell his ability to fill a position in the first place). And certainly when used properly, recruiters can be helpful in accessing open positions before they are advertised. But if you want to find your position faster, you must learn to do what the recruiter does. **You must become your own recruiter.**

IT'S A PRETTY SIMPLE FORMULA

-Develop and cultivate relationships with influencers.

-Develop and cultivate relationships with decision makers.

-Have a plan and be consistent.

All recruiters simply develop relationships with companies on the one hand and with executives seeking new positions on the other, and then connect the two. The good news is that with the strategic plan outlined in this book, you can cut out the recruiter "middleman," so to speak, and develop your own relationships with decision makers and influencers consistently and strategically.

That is how you discover the hidden market. That is how you find the jobs that no one else knows about. And that is how you become top of mind when someone in your industry is looking for a great executive to add to (or head up) their team.

Now that you know the pitfalls to avoid, you're ready to take the very first proactive step in your successful job search: getting your psychology in shape!

THE PSYCHOLOGY OF A SUCCESSFUL SEARCH

03

The Psychology for a Successful Search

Now that you understand the playing field of the executive search world, let's get into something even more important: the psychology of your search.

We are big believers in the concept that we all have the ability to deal with anything we expect. It is those unexpected situations and circumstances that catch us by surprise and sink our confidence or drag us underwater.

This section is dedicated entirely to helping you set expectations for your search, reframe your mindset and prepare you for the ups and downs that are inevitably coming your way. And trust us, your mental conditioning is as important as Olympians conditioning their bodies for the Olympic Games.

In this chapter we are going to cover the most common mental "tripwires" that many executives can get hung up on, and how you can not only avoid them but change your paradigm to one that strengthens your resolve and confidence—in turn helping you land a position faster!

Let's start with several beliefs you need to adopt to empower your current job search mindset.

#1: THE SOONER YOU STOP LOOKING FOR A JOB, THE SOONER YOU'LL FIND ONE

We always tell the clients we work with, "if you want to find a job, stop looking for one." Remember, your job search can't be about you - at least not if you want quicker success. The one thing you can't sell is desperation. When you go into the traditional role of a job seeker, you are automatically putting your search in other people's hands, and let's face it - there is always a hint of desperation that goes along with the process.

Always approach your job search from more of a consultative perspective. That is, network, ask great questions, figure out challenge points, provide solutions, and add value. If you approach your search from this angle, you will not be viewed as a job seeker, but as a valuable asset in the marketplace they are lucky to invest in.

#2: YOU'RE IN CONTROL OF YOUR RESULTS

If you were a child (or had a child) in the 1980's, when you hear, "I have the Power!" you think of He-Man. Well, when it comes to your job search the power doesn't lie with He-Man, nor with the hiring employer. It actually lies with you. Yes…you.

Don't believe me? That may be because you have been searching for a while. Too many executives spend a lot of time finding the right position to apply for. Then they fix up their résumé, write a master cover letter, submit it, and…NOTHING. And every time they don't receive a response, it rips their power away because it is destroying their confidence.

Every time you apply for a position and don't hear anything back, you also destroy your position in the marketplace, thereby discrediting your brand. It doesn't matter if you are the only one who knows it. Your perception is your reality—and your thoughts have consequences.

Instead, you must keep this belief firmly in mind: you are a multi-million dollar product! And you don't sell a multi-million dollar product by submitting a résumé with a cover letter.

The second thing to realize is that employers usually dread hiring more than you dread finding a position. Think about it: it takes time away from their productivity. They are concerned about finding the right fit and whether this new executive will damage their culture. Also, there is significant financial risk if they make the wrong decision. (Remember the Korn Ferry study we talked about in chapter 1 that put the replacement cost of a bad executive hire at $1 million or more.)

It's no wonder that a 2017 report on global human capital trends conducted by Deloitte revealed that talent acquisition is considered "important" or "very important" by 83% of the companies surveyed. .[5]

---

[5] Deloitte Development, LLC, Rewriting the Rules for the Digital Age: 2017 Deloitte Global Human Capital Trends (Deloitte University Press, 2017), p. 39.

A 2016 report by the Association of Executive Search Consultants stated that companies considered the two most important metrics in an executive search were business performance of the successful candidate over time (70%) and tenure of the successful candidate (41%).[6]

Put plainly, most hiring companies are scared of making an expensive mistake—and if you walk in believing you can solve their problem and do a great job for them, they will be thrilled. So if you contact the company or come in for the interview, full of energy and confidence, you will separate yourself from the masses and make their job easier.

Remember, you don't need to be all things to all companies. You just need to be the right version of you for the right company. And you only need one company to buy your multi-million dollar product of YOU.

---

[6] Association of Executive Search Consultants, "Special Edition Report: What's Next for Executive Search and Leadership Consulting," Executive Talent: 7, p. 7.

THE GAME PLAN FOR YOUR SUCCESSFUL JOB SEARCH

04

The Game Plan for Your Successful

You've heard me say it already, and I can't say it enough - **if you are looking for a job, your job is as a sales person, and the product you are selling is YOU. So, just like you would if you were selling any product you need to approach the process methodically and understand that the "job market" is irrelevant and you are in control of your results.**

TAKE CONTROL OF YOUR SEARCH

Too many people enter the realm of unemployment and they just hit the ground running. Fear, anxiety, and the sense of simply needing to do something sets in.

[6] *Association of Executive Search Consultants, "Special Edition Report: What's Next for Executive Search and Leadership Consulting," Executive Talent: 7, p. 7.*

You need to take a step back, take a breath, stop all the activity and figure out what you want for your life today. What do you really want? And why do you want it? Don't ask what you need to do, that will be driven by your why.

You see, people are working now more than they ever have. What's worse is that fulfillment is at an all time low. My hope for you is that you are reading this book to not simply find "a" job, but to find "THE JOB". And you won't find "THE JOB" by accident.

The world of job search brings about so many unknowns and variables in your life. Stress levels typically go through the roof. One of the reasons for this is because you are living in a world of reaction. You see, stress comes from a lack of control. When you feel more in control of events than events are in control of you, the stress will dissipate and you will feel good about what you are doing.

There are few times in life that you feel like you have less control than when you lose your job. That is one of the main reasons we decided to write this book. To give you a roadmap so you knew what you could do to find the perfect opportunity for you. So you would have a system that would put you in control of your results, reduce stress, increase clarity, and expedite results.

In this next section, we will share the 5 step process we use with every one of our clients at the CareerNext Agency to not just find a job, but to find the job that truly fulfills them.

STEP 1: SEEK CLARITY

Habit number 2 in Steven Covey's, The 7 Habits of Highly Effective People is "begin with the end in mind." Your job search is no different than any other business - if you don't know where you want to go, how can you expect to get there?

Your ability to successfully navigate the job search terrain will be based on your clarity around where you want to go and your effectiveness in communicating why you are the best product in the marketplace to fill that position.

While it may seem like an unnecessary step, it is the foundation for everything. However, it's still important to dig deeper. You see, it's important to not simply seek clarity for what you want. Dig deeper! Really connect with WHY you want it. Your "why" will be different than mine or almost anyone else's.

Your "why" is what drives your vision. That's why we have what we call our Vision Map that we walk our clients through. This Vision Map is a series of strategic questions designed to get you to think about your career and life from the perspective of what you want out of both of them and in a way you have probably never fully considered. Unfortunately, I find that most people have a challenging time really diving deep into their "why". The Vision Map helps to pull it out.

Once you are clear on what you want and why you want it, it will lead you to what you need to do. It will empower you to focus on what matters and that focus will help you get the fastest positive result possible. Then at the end, when you land the job, your chances of having a truly fulfilling position will be far greater. You can truly change the direction of your career with this one little step.

On the flip side, having a lack of clarity about your ideal position will have serious negative effects on your search. You won't communicate as clearly with recruiters or other networking opportunities; you will spend a lot of wasted time and energy searching aimlessly online; you'll be chasing after opportunities that won't be fulfilling; and you won't know how to effectively separate yourself from the competition.

Unfortunately, most executives either skip this step or don't give it the attention it deserves and requires to be effective. In all reality, it is the foundation component to everything you do - with both your job search and in business. If you don't have full clarity about what you are looking for, you are almost certainly going to struggle. A former mentor of mine used to say, "if you are searching for nothing, you will find it every time".

GET YOUR MIND RIGHT

If you have watched my YouTube channel, you have heard me say this - "We can deal with anything in life we expect. It's the things we don't expect that throw us off our game".

That's one of the main reasons so many high performing executives struggle when they lose their job. They didn't see it coming. They didn't expect it.

If that is you, don't let it throw you into a whirlwind of reaction. Get your mind right. Focus on your job search like a business. Or if you are a former athlete like me, think of your search like a game or a competition. It's something you are training for.

Remember, just because you were amazing at what you do, doesn't mean you are amazing at finding a job at what you do...and that's okay! Because with the right mindset, plan, and action you can achieve amazing results very quickly.

There are a few key areas you need to focus on to get your mind right:

1. Get REALLY clear on what you want and why you want it.
2. Understand that this process is probably going to be more challenging than you expect.
3. Focus on perfecting the craft of job searching every day (we will cover these areas in steps 2-5).

You can't control how many networking conversations or interviews you get every week. You can only control your activity and own your results. The results will be the byproduct of the activity.

Most of the activities you will be doing for your job search are similar to a sales job - and the product you are selling is you. That is an uncomfortable concept for most people, but it's a concept you will need to embrace to be successful.

Areas To Seek Clarity

While each person will seek clarity in many different areas (some being more unique than others), there are certain core areas I find are essential to have clarity with for a truly successful search.

WHAT ARE YOUR PASSIONS AND INTERESTS?

Identify what you are passionate about. This is different for everybody. You may be passionate about working for a disruptive technology company that challenges the status quo like me. Or maybe you are passionate about working with a company that is sustainable and looking to help the Earth?

Either way, one of the most important elements once you hit the networking and interview stage will be your ability to connect and build relationships. Connecting on shared passions is the most predictable way to achieve a positive result.

Remember, people make decisions emotionally and then validate those decisions with logic. Connecting authentically with someone that has a shared passion will create an instant bond and give you a significant edge.

WHAT ARE YOUR GOALS

Goals can come in many forms. I always find it helpful to break goals down into personal and professional. Create a t-chart. On the left side, write out all of your personal goals. On the right side, write out your professional goals. See how many of those goals overlap.

You will also have a compiled list of your goals you can use to cross reference when you find an opportunity.

Is it important for you to work with a large company that has name recognition? Or maybe you are on the flip side of that coin and prefers working with a smaller company that you can help to build?

How important is upward mobility and future opportunity to you? Is there opportunity for predictable growth inside of the organization? Would this opportunity act as a stepping stone for your ideal position?

How do family dynamics play into your job responsibilities? Do the demands of the job require you to be away from your family the majority of the time? Are you okay with that? Or, are you looking for travel?

HOW DO COMPANY VALUES ALIGN WITH YOURS?

Company values and culture are perhaps the most important element to job selection. Especially for executive level positions. Remember, you are not a rank and file employee. You are being invested in to lead a department, division, region, or even an entire company.

It is absolutely essential that your values are in alignment with the company values. Otherwise, it will only be a matter of time before you feel suffocated, unfulfilled, and unempowered…leaving you ineffective, which can potentially have damaging effects on your career long term.

COMPANY CULTURE

How important is the company culture to you. This is one of the most impactful elements for any company considered on any "best to work for" list.

Is the work environment and structure what you are looking for and comfortable with? Do you relate to the employee base you will be working with?

Is it important to have an office or do you prefer a more communal, open working environment? How much vacation time is given? How involved in the community are they? What else is important to you? Is it important to them?

Side note: *I speak with a lot of people concerned about ageism. Here is the reality, ageism isn't the problem, it's culturism. The hiring manager is simply concerned you won't be a good fit for the culture if you don't connect and relate to their way of doing things. Nothing is more disruptive to the progress of an organization than bringing in a new leader who doesn't naturally fit into the culture. It is your responsibility to identify the culture for any organization you are interviewing with and build a bridge showing how you fit their culture. This is important for everyone, but especially those 45+.*

Going back to the fact that people make decisions emotionally concept, I guarantee this is one of the top items every interviewer will be considering during your interview, so you had better address it.

HOW DOES COMPANY SIZE PLAY INTO YOUR DECISION?

I mentioned this a little earlier when I asked what your goals are. However, I think it is important to really consider what you are looking for. What your skill sets are. And how the value you bring to the table aligns with different sized organizations.

I have seen people who were rock stars at larger companies flounder when they made a shift to a smaller, leaner startup. The same can be said for the inverse of that statement.

How company size and structure plays into your unique abilities should not be underestimated. In fact, you can even find many ways you can build a competitive advantage if your background is in alignment with the size of the organization you are looking to interview with.

DO YOU HAVE ANY GEOGRAPHIC CONSTRAINTS?

Are you looking to find a job in your local area? Are you willing to relocate? Do you need to work remotely? How concerned with the commute time are you?

If you do relocate, will the compensation be ample for cost of living adjustments? Do that have a relocation package?

I know that for many executives with children, this is a really challenging concern. My suggestion is to speak with your spouse and discuss what all the options look like. If you live in a major city, typically the concerns revolve more around commute time and school systems.

Regardless, having clarity around your geographic constraints will enable you to begin a campaign of identifying and targeting ideal companies and decision makers. You can start from an optimal location search and expand out - you will have an A list, B list, and C list for searching.

Your A list will be the perfect match for your geographic desires. This is where you will spend the majority of your time. You want to make sure you exhaust all efforts with all companies and contacts in this region.

Your B list will require some concessions, but will match most of what you are looking for.

Your C list will be comprised of companies that will require significant concession. Think of this as a last resort, but don't ignore it. I am a big believer that you should never say no to a conversation. Especially when interviewing. The worst case scenario is that you get some invaluable practice going through the interview process and don't take the job.

> **One of the most common concerns I hear from job seeking executives is, "I just can't get in front of the right people. I know if I could just talk to the right person, I could land the job. I just don't know who or where they are."**

This is one of the reasons that one of our top services is a research package. The reality is, nobody will be or should be able to sell YOU as well as YOU can sell yourself. However, you can't sell yourself if you are not getting in front of the right people. Not only that, but it takes practice. If you only have a few potential opportunities, that creates anxiety and unpredictable results.

We work with our clients to identify and increase the number of ideal companies where they would be EXCITED to work. Then we expand on that list using industry specific technology which identifies all companies that fit your ideal profile. This helps you build a list of target companies and provides you the key decision makers and contact information to reach them. Imagine how much less anxiety ridden your search would be if you had a list of your ideal companies and the people you could call or network with to land the position. Once you have that list, you simply work it like a salesperson.

INDUSTRY VERTICALS

It is essential that you are clear on the industry verticals where your value is highest. Once you are clear on this, make sure you identify the industry verticals where your skills are most transferable. It's all about building your value proposition.

It doesn't matter what industry you are in today, there are always opportunities for changing industry verticals. We have seen this a lot with the evolution of technology. People who have been in the agency space or telecom (just to name a couple) have been forced to shift their talents to other industries.

No matter your situation, be sure to spend time identifying where your best opportunities exist.

STEP 2: PERSONAL BRANDING & PACKAGING

Now that you have ABSOLUTE CLARITY on what you are looking for, it's time to get into the personal branding and packaging stage. This, sadly, is where most people begin their endeavor. However, as you can now see, it is vital to complete step 1 before building your personal brand.

The question I get all the time is this: "what is required for me to have a successful job search?"

There are the obvious classic documents you need to have:

- Resume
- Cover letter
- Thank you letter

However, there are two other elements that every executive needs to have to stand out from the crowd:

- Executive Proforma
- Optimized LinkedIn profile

I will cover the importance of each one of those items in this section, however there is one other area that is essential for your branding. That is your passion statement. Why? Because your passion statement is as much for you as it is for "them".

YOUR PASSION STATEMENT

Part of knowing what you want is knowing who you are and what you are passionate about. You will have a hard time building a dream without a lot of passion! But remember, passion doesn't come from the head, it comes from the heart. You need to ask yourself, "What am I great at? What do I love to do? What kind of impact do I want to have in life and work?"

Questions such as these will start you on the path to discovering the unique skills and abilities that make you, you. And when you can use those skills and abilities in your job, you're more likely to enjoy your work.

We recommend that all of our clients create what's called a passion statement. This is a declaration, a mantra, that states what you stand for, what you are passionate about, what you want to be known for in your professional life.

There are multiple ways to create a passion statement. We recommend the following.

1. Allow 30 minutes to an hour for the process.

2. Find a quiet place, sit down and take a couple of deep breaths to get centered. Answer these questions.

3. You can either write your answers or simply answer in your mind. The questions fall into three categories.

INTERESTS:

- What activities do you like to pursue outside of work?
- Are there any subjects that you have developed an interest in as an adult?
- What subjects hold particular interests for you?
- Throughout your career, what did you enjoy most about your work?
- List five things that would truly excite you if they were on your calendar for tomorrow.

WORK:

- What activities, functions, or responsibilities do you enjoy that would be part of your ideal job?

- What are your strongest qualifications for your ideal job? What strengths do you have that you would make you great at this position?

- What are you great at doing? What talents, interests and qualifications do you possess that make you great at your job? (Hint: This is the time to brag about yourself.)

MISSION:

- Do you feel you have a mission, a purpose for your life? What is it?

- What kind of impact do you want to have at work and in life? What kind of contribution do you want to make to others or the world?

4. Once you have your answers to these questions in your mind, write a few sentences that describe who you are at your best. Make your description something that excites you and makes you passionate

HERE ARE A COUPLE OF EXAMPLES OF A PASSION STATEMENT:

"I am an accomplished visionary change agent, business partner; top-level solution provider and industry thought leader that constantly delivers hard driving, steadfast solutions."

"I am an exceptional leader and inspirer of top-performing teams, guiding them to exceed all goals in creative and innovative ways. The solutions we provide add massive value to our customers, our company and society as a whole."

5. Feel free to write multiple versions of your passion statement and to keep fine-tuning it until it feels right. Try reading your final version aloud a few times to make sure it works for you. Then write it out and put it somewhere you can see it daily!

Remember, you can't be all things to all people. An important part of your passion statement is making a stand on what you stand for—what you are passionate about. That is what will sell you to employers. More importantly, it will help you find a position that will help you be excited to go to work each day.

Before going on to the next chapter, we encourage you to spend a little time thinking about what really makes you tick. What could you do that would get you out of bed every morning excited to make an impact? When you have that dialed in and believe it in your core, you will feel the power shift and realize that you are a tremendous potential asset.

Once you have your passion statement dialed in, you need to learn how to articulate it effectively. Only then do you start to reach out to decision makers.

MAKE YOUR DREAM BIG ENOUGH TO MAKE YOU UNCOMFORTABLE

Once you have your passion statement and a picture of your ideal executive position, you're ready to dream big—probably bigger than you've done before. Recognize that a good dream is certain to make you a bit uncomfortable and that's good!

It's scary to dream. Change is scary. But what is even scarier is working the rest of your career in an unfulfilling, non-impactful position. You are reading this book for a reason. You want more from your life. As Henry David Thoreau once said, "It's not enough to be busy. So too are the ants. The question is: What are we busy about?"

A dream needs to mean something to you. It needs to be big. Don't sell yourself short. Few make it to the level you already have. Of course you can take it to the next level!

I once heard someone say, "Make your dream so big that when it comes true, you can't take credit for it." When you begin with a dream as your destination, you set the course for success.

With a picture of your ultimate destination (your ideal position) and your passion statement firmly in mind, and a willingness to dream big enough to be uncomfortable, you're ready to build your brand so you can effectively sell the multimillion-dollar product of you!

REQUIRED DOCUMENTS FOR A SUCCESSFUL BRANDING CAMPAIGN

It is key to understand the documents and tools you need to run a successful branding campaign as a job seeker. I gave a list earlier about the five items you need for a successful campaign:

- *Resume*
- *Cover letter*
- *Thank you letter*
- *Executive Proforma*
- *Optimized LinkedIn profile*

However, it's not just about having all of those tools. It's how you use them. In the following section, I will cover each item required for your branding campaign.

RESUME

In a world where technology dominates, you still need to have a good old fashion resume. You want to make sure you have this in all formats: print (hard copy), PDF, & Word format.

However, while having a top notch resume is required, it is also the most misunderstood of all the marketing tools. Most people think the key to their success is to have an amazing resume. Nothing could be further from the truth.

Remember, people don't hire resumes. In fact, I will tell you this - if you are leading with your resume, you are doing it wrong. You see, the resume isn't a marketing document. It's a historical record of your body of work. It is the proof that will back up their decision to move forward with hiring you.

Too often I hear horror stories of executives missing out on opportunity because their outreach strategy consisted of finding a recruiter/company/decision maker and sending them their resume. There is almost no more certain way to get turned down. **Unless they directly ask for you to send your resume, DON'T SEND IT.**

Leading with your resume is a selfish act. It's basically you telling them that all you care about is getting a job so you can have a paycheck. Remember, your job search isn't about you. It is about the hiring company and how you can solve their problems. You will rarely be able to authentically articulate that by leading with your resume.

COVER LETTER

When they do finally ask for your resume or if you are submitting to a job posting (which will be roughly 5-10% of your search), you will want to make sure to include a pattern interrupt cover letter.

Why do I call it a pattern interrupt cover letter? Because you have 7 seconds to capture their attention. You will submit this customized cover letter with each resume you submit. This is your chance to make an instant connection. They are in the habit of looking at generically written, poorly formatted cover letters and resumes - then discarding them into the recycle bin.

You need to create an instant connection. Make sure you do your research and use the cover letter to create a bridge.

THANK YOU LETTER

The thank you letter (or email) is a lost art. I will talk about it later during the interview section, but you should always follow up an interview with a personalized thank you letter. This letter should thank them for their consideration, express your excitement for the opportunity, and list a couple reasons you feel like you would be the best fit for the position (how you can solve their problems).

The thank you letter is one of those intangibles that will help differentiate you from the pack. It is another touch point that helps you to solidify your brand and stay top of mind with the decision maker or panel.

EXECUTIVE PROFORMA

You hear me say it all the time on my podcast, "no company is going to hire you, they are going to *invest* in you". That's why we call this document an executive proforma.

After all, if you have ever purchased a mutual fund or other types of investment, there is always an investment proforma that shows past performance and results. It is a marketing document focusing on only the things the investor needs to know to look deeper.

Every person looking to obtain any sort of leadership position needs to have an Executive Proforma. It is a one-sheet document that gives a snapshot of your past results. It uses statistics, graphics, charts, images, and quantifiable data to increase the rate of response.

The purpose of the Executive Proforma is to be your main marketing document in place of how you would normally use your resume. You put up a PDF on your LinkedIn profile, you share it with your network, recruiters, etc...

Remember, you still need to make sure you are not simply blasting this out and spamming people with it, but using this document as a follow up to an initial conversation will dramatically help you increase your odds of getting to the next level of the process.

OPTIMIZED LINKEDIN PROFILE

LinkedIn is an area that most people struggle with. They either don't want to have a profile, or they have a profile and are not using it to its full potential.

LinkedIn is so important to your executive job search that I dedicated an entire section to it later in the book. But for now, let me say this (you will understand later).

LinkedIn has become the access point to decision makers. It is the platform you can use to build your brand. VIRTUALLY EVERY decision maker will look at your profile and use that experience as a tool in their decision making process. Not putting the effort into having an optimized LinkedIn profile puts you on the borderline of career suicide.

The older you are, the more important it is. Remember, being relevant and having an established brand on LinkedIn can help ease a lot of concerns about your age and cultural fit for the hiring organization.

I will go into detail later about HOW to build your brand, stand out, and be discovered on LinkedIn.

Now that you have the five areas to focus on building your brand, I am going to get into what you need to consider as you build out your brand inside of those tools.

Your Brand —
Know What You Are Selling

Your job search is essentially a sales job, and at the executive level you are selling a multimillion-dollar product. They may not pay you multi-millions of dollars (or they might), but that is certainly the value you bring to the table for your prospective new company.

You don't sell a $1 million dollar Bugatti the same way you sell a Toyota Camry. You don't sell a $10 million dollar house the same way you sell a $400,000 house. And you certainly don't land an executive level position the same way you landed your first or second job out of college!

You must understand your value proposition and know that you are an extremely valuable product and asset in the marketplace. Once you do, you can learn how to sell that product effectively.

WHAT IS YOUR BRAND?

Start by making sure your brand is recognizable and differentiated from the "generic brands" that you are competing against. In your executive search, being known for something is half the battle. It's like a political campaign. We believe that one of the reasons Donald Trump was elected president of the United States is that he is a master of branding. Love him or hate him, you knew of him long before he became the 45th president of the United States, and his particular brand was very clear. Developing your brand is one of the most overlooked yet important areas of getting ready for your search. It goes back to the concept of starting with the end in mind. You can't sell yourself in the market until you can effectively articulate your brand and value proposition. Once you know your brand, you will communicate it using classical tools like a résumé, cover letters, executive proforma, executive bio, etc.—essentially your "marketing packet."

Simon Sinek did an amazing TED Talk on how great leaders inspire action. (If you haven't read Simon Sinek's book, Start With Why, or seen his 20-minute TED Talk, you should pause reading this book right now and go watch it.) The summary of his talk in context of your search is simple: Everyone knows "what" they do. Fewer people (albeit most at the executive level) know "how" to do it effectively. But only a small percentage of people know "why" they are doing it.

Surprisingly, even at the executive level, this is the Achilles heel of communicating your value proposition. Until you can resonate with your "why," you won't be able to communicate why you are the best fit for any company with any sort of passion.

The great part about truly knowing your why is that it takes job hunting off the table. Once you are in tune with your why, settling for any old job will simply be unacceptable for you.

> **REMEMBER,**
> You can't be all things to all people. The surest way to stand out from the crowd is to develop your brand and then find a company that fits you, not the other way around. Trust me, it's out there.

QUESTIONS TO ASK YOURSELF AS YOU ARE DEVELOPING YOUR BRAND

In the last chapter you created a passion statement. Now you'll use both that statement and the thinking process that developed it to shape your personal brand.

Answer the following three questions

1. WHAT ARE YOU SELLING?

What are you as a multi-million dollar "product" bringing to the table that will help you stand out to your targeted companies?

- *Are you selling your ability to build a team?*
- *To double sales?*
- *To reign in costs?*
- *To reorganize and/or streamline a department, division, or company?*

- To increase profits?
- To implement new technology?
- To open up locations or operations in new cities or countries?
- To develop and implement new strategic plans or direction?
- To create better communication and cooperation between divisions?
- To improve their core business?
- To expand into new markets?
- To create new product lines?

> **REMEMBER,**
>
> Ultimately what you are selling is your ability to solve a company's problems—even the problems they don't know they have. Come up with a list of three or four "core competencies" that you have successfully demonstrated and that you enjoy using.

2. WHO ARE YOU?

John Maxwell once wrote,

"People don't care how much you know until they know how much you care. But once they find out how much you care, you'd better know something."

Needing to "know something" is a given at your level. Communicating WHO you are beyond what you know is going to play a huge part of your success in landing your next executive position.

What makes you tick? What interests do you have outside of work? What talents do you like using? What great qualities do you bring to the table? You can use your passion statement to help you answer this question.

3. WHAT SETS YOU APART?

This is definitely where you need your passion statement. Remember, landing your next position is a sales job. And if you think about most things you have ever purchased, the enthusiasm of your salesperson probably played a big part in your decision.

Authentic enthusiasm is virtually impossible to fake. We all seem to be aware when salespeople are BS-ing us. On the flip side, we remember the unique individuals who were selling something they were so passionate about that you knew they couldn't wait to come to work. They truly believed what they were doing and selling was going to make a positive impact in the lives of whomever they were selling to. You need to be that person when it comes to selling your brand!

Remember, passion sells.

If you can't get excited about you, how can you expect anyone else to? After all, there is so much about you they don't even know. Lead with passion and fill the rest in after. The hiring organization will guide you in filling in all the technical aspects by asking the appropriate questions.

When it comes to developing your brand, get out of your head and into your heart. Your why does not exist in your head—it resides in your heart. You will have a chance to talk about your intellect (the what and how you do what you do), but everyone knows that stuff. If you want to stand apart from the crowd, you need to focus on WHY

Begin A Personal Branding Campaign

The reason most executive job seekers are horrible brand-builders is that they are blindsided by the sense of urgency brought on by the process of modern day job hunting. You can't build a brand reactively. **You must separate personal promotion (brand building) from job hunting altogether.**

Traditional job hunting is a frustrating process. Spending hundreds of hours sifting through the fool's gold on internet job boards is a recipe for failure. Submitting your resume to recruiters thinking they will somehow magically be representing the position you are looking for is like finding a needle in a haystack. You are just as likely to find your husband/wife/soulmate on *spouseofmydreams.com* (kidding, not a real website). Sure, you may go on a couple dates, but they aren't likely to go anywhere.

The driven executive becomes so focused on pursuing the job that he sometimes misses the much bigger picture. A successful personal brand-building campaign must be conducted separately from job hunting.

Don't limit your branding campaign to the people you think can help you get a job. Instead, focus on building a clear personal brand for everyone in your network and everyone who happens to cross your information.

The good news is that with LinkedIn, personal branding has never been so easy. You can embark on a personal promotion campaign to your warm network - having personal conversations (networking) and giving them awareness of your availability in the marketplace with clear calls to action (how they can help you).

The second portion of bulking up your brand is building your expert status on LinkedIn so you will be more attractive to the people who you want to know you, but don't know you yet.

You see, personal branding is a two pronged approach. You should never do just one exclusively. And while you should always begin with your warm network, you need to think of it like a sales pipeline (without being a used car salesman/woman).

A good networking conversation is not about reaching out to people you know to have a cup of coffee and talk about the weather. It's about connecting with them. Remember, people make decisions emotionally. Go into the conversation, connect with them on a personal level, see what value you can add to their life, and have a clear call to action on how they can help you. If you do this right, you should have no issues coming away with two or three solid referrals.

When networking is done properly inside of your personal branding campaign, you will find that reaching out to only 20-25 of your network contacts will make you more busy than you know what to do with.

Remember, you are a multimillion-dollar product and you have great value to add to any company. You want to make sure your brand is recognizable and your value is clear. I will dive deeper into how to leverage LinkedIn to build your brand

Use Social Media (Especially LinkedIn) to Build Your Brand

Anytime you are curious or skeptical about something, what do you do? You Google it! Well, you can be certain that anyone you connect with about any type of executive opportunity will be doing an Internet search on YOU.

Companies and recruiters are actively using Google and social media to find out more about executive candidates. In 2012, the recruiting software firm JobVite.com polled over 800 employers to ask if they used social networks and media (including LinkedIn, Facebook, and Twitter) to identify and recruit talent. And 92% indicated that they did![7]

Any wonder that we tell candidates they must modernize the way they seek professional career advancement to include creating a strong brand for themselves online?

---

[7] "Jobvite Social Recruiting Survey Finds Over 90% of Employers Will Use Social Recruiting in 2012," 9 July 2012, https://www.jobvite.com/news_item/jobvite-social-recruiting-survey-finds-90-employers-will-use-social-recruiting-2012/.

If used the right way, social media and the Internet can be valuable allies in your job search. Why?

- *Career seekers can now access contacts 24/7 in the convenience of their home, office, or local coffee shop. No more attending a seven AM breakfast event where only 20 people show up. Instead, you have the opportunity to interact with thousands of people all over the globe at the touch of a keystroke.*

- *Remember: the first thing a decision maker thinks when bringing a job to market is, "Who do I know that would be a good fit for this position?" Those same decision makers are using the Internet and social media to check on those people and to verify their impressions with more information. (It is well known that top ranking executive recruiters search the Internet thoroughly before presenting a candidate to a company.)*

- *Most companies want executives who are "current"—that is, aware of trends and up on the latest tools and skills. Making sure the information about you online and on social media is up to date and represents you accurately and favorably makes you appear more "tech savvy."*

But there's a reason to be very careful about your social media presence. A 2017 CareerBuilder study found that 54% of employers declined to hire someone because of content they found on the candidate's social media profile, such as: inappropriate videos, photos, or information; discriminatory comments; confidential information about a past employer; bad-mouthing their previous company or fellow employees; even having an unprofessional screen name.[8]

The lesson here is that anything and everything online should be considered part of your professional brand. Monitoring your online and social media presence regularly will ensure that your brand and value proposition represents you well.

---

[8] "Number of Employers Using Social Media to Screen Candidates at All-Time High, Finds Latest CareerBuilder Study," 15 June 2017, http://press.careerbuilder.com/2017-06-15-Number-of-Employers-Using-Social-Media-to-Screen-Candidates-at-All-Time-High-Finds-Latest-CareerBuilder-Study.

BASIC PRINCIPLES FOR INTERNET AND SOCIAL MEDIA SUCCESS

Building your brand must be an ongoing effort—before, during, and after you are looking for a new executive position. And a successful social media brand building campaign must be developed and executed separately from conventional job networking.

Here are five principles to follow as you create a strong Internet and social media brand.

1. BE SEARCHABLE.

If there isn't much about you online, that can be as much of a red flag for employers as having too little. Make sure your Internet presence communicates a clear message about who you are and what you have to offer. Focus on what key players need to see in your profile or online presence to make the right impression.

2. BE LASER FOCUSED.

When developing your Internet and social media brand, you don't want to be on every platform possible. You will spread yourself way too thin and be ineffective with all of the platforms. To make it easier to build your online brand, choose one primary platform based upon the profile of your target market or community. (For most executives, that is LinkedIn.)

3. BE SEEN AS AN EXPERT IN YOUR FIELD.

Focus on what key players need to see to get the right impression. When recruiters and executive search firms search for information on candidates, they often will look for people who wrote or were quoted in industry-relevant articles, or who have spoken at conferences, or have distinguished themselves in some way in their professional capacity.

Engaging with other industry experts online can help you strengthen your brand. Commenting on articles posted by leading figures, for example, or sharing their articles on your LinkedIn account, or writing a guest post for an industry leader's blog can increase your visibility. And you might consider writing your own articles and posts as part of your LinkedIn presence.

4. BE CONSISTENT.

Getting visible on the Internet requires a strategy and a thematic message. Your message needs to be consistent with respect to who you are, what you do, and why it matters. It must be consistent across all platforms as well and should contain only what you want potential employers and recruiters to see.

You also must execute that strategy consistently. Make sure are proactively putting out content online that tells the story of who you are. Just having a LinkedIn page (that you never update) is not enough. You are a high level executive. The more positive positioning you can have online, the better you will stand out against the competition.

5. BE PATIENT.

Just like it takes time to develop a deep friendship in life, it will take time to build a strong online presence online and develop a community who knows who you are. We would advise starting now if you haven't already.

CHOOSE YOUR PLATFORM

Now, you don't need to spend hours per day online building your Internet and social media presence. But you should choose one or two platforms to make your Internet "home," and then make it part of your schedule to engage on whatever platform(s) you choose on a daily or weekly basis.

While most executives prefer to use LinkedIn, there are benefits to developing a brand on Twitter, Facebook, or via a personal website or blog. We'll discuss all of these in this chapter, with the primary focus being the "800-pound gorilla": LinkedIn.

LINKEDIN

Did you know there are more than 467 million people on LinkedIn? That's over 100 million more than the entire population of the U.S.!

Think of LinkedIn as one of the most up-to-date databases of professionals in the world. Almost 90% of the human resource executives and executive recruiters that we work with indicate that they routinely scour profiles of LinkedIn members looking for potential candidates.

In fact, not being a member of LinkedIn can be detrimental in a job search. Company representatives have told our clients that candidates not on LinkedIn will not be considered for an interview. Bottom line: you need to be on LinkedIn, and your presence there needs to be professional and effective.

The two primary functions of LinkedIn are networking and brand building. Once you have created a profile, you want to start doing both immediately.

Free or Premium LinkedIn Subscription?

Whether or not you use the free or premium version of LinkedIn depends on how you decide to leverage LinkedIn as a tool.

One of the significant benefits of having a premium account is an enhanced search tool that can make connecting with the right people faster, more effective, and more efficient.

With the paid version, you also can receive InMail messages from people you are not already connected to. InMail messages are sent directly to another LinkedIn member you're not connected with. This makes your ability to reach people you are not connected with easier.

The most important part of a premium LinkedIn account is that you can utilize it as a CRM. You can keep track of contacts and make notes about who you have reached out to, follow ups, conversations, and more. You also can use it to contact recruiters that may help you in your search.

While a LinkedIn Premium account is not cheap, it is well worth it when you consider it is probably costing you over $800 per day to be out of work and looking for a job. While you used to be able to get by with the free version, your effectiveness will be far greater with a premium account.

LinkedIn Sales Navigator

This may seem a bit counter-intuitive, but Sales Navigator is the best LinkedIn Premium option as a job seeker. While they have subscriptions that are titled more for job seekers or recruiters, you don't want to handle your job search like a job seeker. You want to handle it like a sales process and while Sales Navigator is a bit more expensive than other premium options, it is worth its weight in gold.

It enables you to do specific company searches, get notified of updates inside targeted organizations and expand your ability to connect with key decision makers unlike any other option.

We discuss in detail how to best leverage Sales Navigator within our LinkedIn Networking Academy online course.

Networking on LinkedIn

LinkedIn is, at its core, a networking platform for connecting business people. It is organized around people you know (1st degree connections), people they know (2nd degree connections), and the people those second degree connections know (3rd degree connections). To use LinkedIn effectively, you want to maximize your first degree connections so they can link you to the second and third degree people who might lead you to your next position.

Start by importing all of your contacts from Outlook, Gmail, etc. into your LinkedIn account, and then invite them to link with you or accept their invitations. When you look at the LinkedIn profiles of people in your network, you may find out some information about them that you never knew before, including professional skills, outside interests, business awards and recognition, and so on.

When you look at the profiles of your network, look over their connections and see if there is someone you would like them to connect you with. If so, ask your contact to introduce you over the platform. (You also should see if you know someone that they may want to be introduced to, and then make an offer to do so.)

Whenever people invite you to connect with them, review their profile and see (1) if they are connected with one of your current network, and (2) if they are the kind of connection you would like to have. Many people put out requests to connect with anyone and everyone on LinkedIn, and that's fine—but there are some individuals that you don't necessarily want as one of your connections because of their reputation.

Be willing to connect with a wide range of people and businesses, but don't be afraid to say no either. You will be evaluated by others (i.e., potential employers) by the quality of your network, so do what you can to keep the quality high.

How To Get People To Engage With Your Profile On LinkedIn

There are three things every person will see on your page when they visit your LinkedIn profile. When someone searches your name on LinkedIn and your page shows up in the results, they will see your profile photo, your current headline, and the description for your current position.

Once they click on your name and go to your page, they will see your header photo, profile photo, current headline, and the first few lines of your summary. **If you want to have an effective LinkedIn profile, it is essential for you to have all of these elements of your profile dialed in.**

The first thing to do is very basic: *have a professional looking profile photo*. This is the first impression of your brand and it is essential that it speaks to who you are. Make sure it is clean and only of you.

The second thing is to *make sure your headline talks about who you are and what you do*. This can be a bit tricky and take some thought, but it is worth it. Your headline is keyword sensitive, so make sure if anyone is looking for someone with your skills, the keywords associated with your skill sets are in your headline.

Key point: NEVER put "Currently Seeking Opportunity" or anything of that nature as your headline.

The perspective you need to have when writing your headline is to think of the way you would describe yourself at a networking event. The headline needs to speak to who you are and be catchy to your target audience.

My advice is to think about the type of decision maker you are trying to reach, and what you would say to him or her at a networking event. Once again, it is not about reaching everyone, but reaching the right person.

When someone goes to your LinkedIn profile page, underneath your headline *they will see the first few lines of your summary*. It is important for these first few lines are impactful. It is typically best practice for those first few lines to be an extension of your headline. You are looking to draw your visitor in and have them click the "read more" tab below.

HERE'S AN EXAMPLE OF A GREAT HEADLINE AND EXECUTIVE SUMMARY:

Adam Johnson

CEO/CFO/COO and Investor in Early-Stage Companies

Startup Organizational Development · Disruptive Products & Innovation • M&A Target Identification

Strong financial and operational executive with venture capital and technology background. Specializes in identifying and investing in new market opportunities, M&A, and new product development across Europe, North America (NA), Asia, and Africa.

Robust experience with disruptive technology, startups, and product innovation, e.g. raising capital, developing infrastructure, and scaling company for growth. Expert in negotiating strategic partnerships and managing investors/stakeholders, bankers, and Boards. Directs accelerated speed to market strategies through organic growth and acquisitions to increase shareholder value.

Extensive experience developing and commercializing revolutionary digital media solutions, including OTT video and video advertising sectors. Deep understanding of Smart TVs, streaming devices (e.g. Roku/Chromecast), and video encoding workflows.

Another important thing that most people overlook is the banner photo. LinkedIn gives you the ability to have one, so not taking advantage of it is foolish and quite frankly, looks unprofessional. This banner needs to speak about who you are. It doesn't need to be professional in scope, but it always needs to look professionally done.

We always make sure that our clients have their LinkedIn profiles optimized and set up correctly. It can certainly be a lot of work, but it is worth it. After all, almost every position you are looking for will pass through LinkedIn at some point in time. You want to make sure you are discoverable and clearly a great candidate for that opportunity.

Building Your Brand on LinkedIn

While many people continue to struggle, dumping hundreds of wasted hours into LinkedIn, others are thriving. How? There is, in fact, a very predictable hiring process where you can get a much better output of results with much less input of time: be known, be liked, be trusted, be hired. You can use LinkedIn to help you in every step of that journey.

> **First**, if you already have a good relationship with someone, being active on LinkedIn and keeping your profile up to date is a great way of staying top of mind. If a position comes open, it may help you enter the running while it is still in the hidden market.
>
> **Second**, even if the decision maker doesn't know you well or at all, they can now circumvent traditional job boards or do their own recruiting using LinkedIn. The reason this is so important is because almost every job will go through LinkedIn on some level before reaching a job board, recruiter, or headhunter. Remember, any hiring employer is going to have a pretty significant expense if they need to place the position with a recruiter or headhunter. LinkedIn gives employers the ability to circumvent the need for recruiters.
>
> **Third**, we have talked a lot about branding and the fact that people want to work with people they know, like, and trust. There is no better bang for your buck than doing this on LinkedIn. Let's talk about how LinkedIn can help you with this process.

#1: Be Known

To utilize LinkedIn effectively you must be active. Do everything LinkedIn suggests: Have a full and complete profile. Connect with people that have synergy with you and your industry. Remain active with your network on LinkedIn. (However, do your best to keep online activities outside the hours of 9 to 5, the hours when most people are at work.)

Being known via LinkedIn follows the same rules as having a conversation with someone. If you spend 80% of the time "listening" to others on LinkedIn and 20% talking about yourself, you will be more effective. And online, you listen to others by engaging with their content.

By liking and sharing people's posts, articles, or any other content, you are telling them two things. First, you care and they are making an impact on you. Second, that there is a synergy between you. And most importantly, you are keeping yourself top of mind, not just for them, but also for anyone else who has liked or engaged with the same content.

Bonus point #1: Make sure you are connecting with people whom you see consistently engaging with the same content as you.

Bonus point #2: The objective of every online interaction is to take the relationship offline with a phone call, Skype call, or even a meeting over coffee if geography permits.

#2: Be Liked

What you do for others, others will do for you. To have an effective LinkedIn presence, you need to do four things.

> **First**, share other people's relevant content. This is the easiest and fastest way to add value to your network and to also get the pulse of who is truly the most synergistic with you.
>
> However, be sure to have proper expectation management with sharing content. Anytime you share content online, it will be slow building. You may start off with no responses or likes, then one or two, and so on. The key is consistency. Remember, you don't need 100 people to like your post—only that one right person for it to be effective.
>
> **Second**, create and share your own content. This is a bit more time-consuming but will really help you build a following and stand out from the crowd. This is all about your branding. Create relevant content for who you are, what you do, and why you do it.

Third, have an opinion. You can't be all things to all people. Remember, you are not trying to get everyone to like you: you are getting the right people to like you. Make sure you stand for something.

Fourth, have personal engagement. If people hire people they know, like, and trust, the surest way to be known and hopefully liked is to engage and be engaging. When someone makes a comment on anything you post, respond and engage with them. Create conversation. This is a key component to building likeability and trust on LinkedIn.

#3: Be Trusted

Let's face it: we live in a hyper-skeptical world. Your job on LinkedIn is to convert those skeptics into raving fans of your brand. Luckily, building trust on LinkedIn is a really simple equation:

$$(QUALITY\ CONTENT + ENGAGEMENT) \times TIME = Trust$$

Content and engagement are how you build relationships online. When you do that consistently over time, trust multiplies. You will find that once you hit the tipping point, you will become an expert in your field. Then people won't just trust you; they will become your fans.

Position yourself as the thought leader that people come to for advice. There is a ton of value being perceived as an expert of a thought leader in your field on LinkedIn. (One of the major things we help all of our clients with is getting their LinkedIn profile set up and prepare them to become thought leaders.)

As long as you are consistent with your content and messaging, it will all come together. Being in front of people consistently will help them to feel like they know you. Once you reach that level, the world of opportunity is completely open and you will have a tribe of raving fans behind you.

#4: Be Hired

If you are looking to get hired from a contact on LinkedIn, there are a couple of essential things essential to consider.

First, everything must be done with specific intent. Make sure the content you share and create is relevant to your industry and makes you stand out from the crowd.

Second, people need to know how to reach you. Be sure to have your email and phone number easily accessible for anyone who wants to call you. Be responsive and professional with those who reach out.

Expectation management note: Whenever you make your information (like phone number) public, you will receive calls every now and then from people who are little bit "spammy." Don't let that deter you from the great contacts that need that information to reach you. Sure, they can use Messaging on LinkedIn, but nothing beats a phone number.

Using LinkedIn to Look for Work When You're Still Employed

One of the items recruiters look for is people who are becoming more active with their LinkedIn profile, as it is an indicator that you are looking to join the job market. If you are currently employed, you need to be careful. If you don't handle your LinkedIn account properly, you can trigger a red flag for your current employer.
If you are currently employed but looking to enter the job market, follow this link and this advice: https://youtu.be/TasDysjTN_k

1. *Log on to your LinkedIn account.*

2. *Go To: ME > Settings & Privacy > Sharing Profile Edits. Set this to NO.*

3. *Under "Who Can See Your Connections": Change to ONLY ME (and keep it as "only me" during your executive job search)*

4. *Turn "Group Join" Notifications OFF. Joining a lot of new groups also can trigger your employer's interest.*

If you are not employed, this isn't anything you should be too concerned with. Just change the "sharing profile edits" until your profile is where you want it to be.

Make the Most of LinkedIn's Social Selling Index

One of the main reasons people struggle with using LinkedIn is that they are "job hunting." Remember, you are not job hunting: you are job sowing. You are campaigning, building your brand, exposing people to who you are and why it matters to them.

To see how well you are building your brand, finding the right people to connect with, and engaging effectively, LinkedIn has what they call a social selling index, and it's something that everyone has tied to their LinkedIn account.

There are four areas that LinkedIn focuses on for you. These areas walk you through the best practices LinkedIn says you need to be focused on to effectively sell yourself on the platform (which is exactly what you are trying to do).

AREA #1: ESTABLISH YOUR PROFESSIONAL BRAND

AREA #2: FIND THE RIGHT PEOPLE

Make sure you are connecting with a minimum of three people in your industry per day for effectiveness.

AREA #3: ENGAGE WITH INSIGHTS

Content that you have created or shared. This is all about establishing yourself as a thought leader.

AREA #4: BUILD RELATIONSHIPS

LinkedIn is about building one-to-one relationships—ultimately with decision makers as much as possible. However, remember that the ultimate goal is to take your relationship offline, either on the phone or ideally face-to-face.

You can use this link to access your own social selling index: https://www.linkedin.com/sales/ssi

The average SSI score is 45 out of 100. Tracking your score and always working to improve it is a great barometer to see if you are focusing on the right activities no LinkedIn.

We've covered LinkedIn thoroughly, but there are other ways to establish a powerful brand online. Next we'll talk about Twitter, Facebook, and your own website or blog.

If you are overwhelmed (as many are) at the thought of needing to find your position using LinkedIn, I understand. LinkedIn can be your greatest tool or your greatest waste of time. That's why we created the LinkedIn Networking Academy. It's an online video course that coaches you through every nuance of every topic discussed in this section. Check it out at www.CareerNextAgency.com.

Twitter

You might be surprised how many recruiters and senior executives are using Twitter. This platform has fast developed into the ultimate utility to connect directly with recruiters and employees at companies you're targeting. By conducting Twitter searches, following recruiters on your account and using the "@" sign to communicate with them on occasion, you will begin to find out a lot about them and their companies.

Before you follow anyone on Twitter, you will need to have a finished profile. This means you must have a short bio, the location where you're from, and a link to a site that recruiters can go to for more information, e.g., your LinkedIn page, personal website or blog. It's fairly simple. Go to Twitter.com and jump right in! It's fast, free and fun.

Once you're on Twitter, search for your target contacts. Follow and retweet them. Also look for your target companies, job search experts, and job boards. They're tweeting job openings, offering advice and resources, and much more. An active Twitter presence shows you're an up-to-date, social media-savvy candidate.

Facebook

If you think Facebook is only for teenagers who love to post personal content, think again: the average Facebook user is almost 42 years old! And there are effective ways to network via Facebook without discrediting your brand.

If you're in the over-45 age demographic, we suggest you explore Facebook.com as another resource or media to expose your professional candidacy. More than one billion users can't all be wrong! You can't afford not to have a presence here. Go to Facebook.com to get started. BUT...be sure that your Facebook profile is used exclusively for the purposes of your career endeavors. You can create separate professional and personal pages on Facebook; just be aware that whatever you post on the personal side may be searchable by someone looking for your professional page. So never post anything you don't want the world to see—and make sure your review your Privacy settings regularly so your data won't be used in ways you don't want.

Personal Website, Blogs and Online Media

Many people nowadays have a personal website. If this is you, congratulations! This personal platform can be used as part of your job search.

Before I entered the career coaching space, I owned an internet marketing agency helping small business owners build their businesses online. We would identify their avatar (ideal client), build their brand to that market, and create a marketing campaign to sell their product or service to their target market.

Does that sound familiar? You are essentially a business of one. Your job is to make sure you use your personal site to enhance your brand. Use your personal site to feature quality content that is connected to your industry or area of expertise as an executive. Having your own website with a blog or vlog will help position you as an expert and thought leader in your field.

Consider ways that you can use your website or blog to build your brand. Post content on a regular basis. Invite your network or others you admire to be guest bloggers for you (they write a blog post and you publish it on your web page). Be a guest blogger for others in your field. If your target people blog or write articles on sites, post comments that reinforce your brand and promise of value. Post links to articles and information from industry experts, and comment on them yourself.

Above all, if you have a website or blog, make SURE that you reply to any comments that people leave. The Internet and social media are all about engagement. The more engaged you are with quality content and comments, the more you will be top of mind with the contacts who can help you.

Whatever platform you choose, ensure that you have a disciplined, on-going, daily connection strategy. Each one offers its own benefits. Decide how much time you can allot to social networking and which platforms work best for you. Then get busy establishing your brand and connecting with the people who can offer you a great executive position!

As important as your brand is, knowing your market is equally important. Now that you have your personal branding campaign underway, you need to know how to identify and target ideal companies and key decision makers. That's the topic of our next chapter.

STEP 3: IDENTIFY AND TARGET IDEAL COMPANIES & PEOPLE

As important as knowing what your brand is, knowing the market you want to reach is equally important. It consists of the people and companies that can offer or create the position you want. These people are the investors, the "buyers", if you will, of the multimillion-dollar product of you.

You need to know not only who your buyers are but also WHERE they are. It's essential to understand where your potential buyers can be found. Being clear on that will help you dial in your message appropriately and target your efforts to reach the people that will matter most in your job search.

Your search for your buyers will encompass three areas:
- *The cold (or open) market*
- *Your network (or your warm market)*
- *The networks of your friends and professional associates (potential connections)*

Think of your executive search as a startup company. All you need to do is land your first client...that's it! That client may come from your network, the cold market, or the networks of your friends and professional associates. It makes no difference so long as the opportunity is exactly what you are looking for.

However, it is important to have a process in place for each area where your potential buyers are congregating (the cold market, your network, and the networks of your friends and professional associates). The process with each area will be slightly different because the level of relationship is different.

> I mentioned it earlier, the two points of contention which lead to the greatest problems for job seekers is knowing how to find the right companies (because they are not listed) and connecting with key decision makers inside of those companies. That's why it is essential to start with a few core companies where you would be excited to work and then reverse engineer the key attributes of those companies to expand the list of companies. It's one of the most important aspects to a successful search and one of the more challenging things to do.

THE COLD MARKET

This is where most people tend to start their job search—simply because they know of no other way. They've been deluded into the belief that spending hours on Internet job boards or chasing appointments with recruiters and headhunters is the best way to get a great job.

Remember, to find what you are looking for you need to remove yourself from the mindset of job hunting. Flip the table, go hire yourself an employer. Your search can't be about "available jobs." There is no shortage of opportunity in the world. There is a serious shortage of quality, or at least people who can articulately communicate their value proposition and "why."

You are different. You have that part down (or are at least working on it). So why would you go about your executive search the way 99% of executives do?

While the cold market contains all companies that can offer you an executive position suited to your skills, abilities and ambitions, you might as well start your search by identifying a few great employers. **Make a "top 10" list of companies you would like to work for and why you think they would be a good fit.** By identifying 10 "ideal buyers," you can start to see more clearly both your requirements for a great job and the value proposition you will bring to the table.

This is an important distinction. Notice I didn't say go out and find the top 10 positions available online in your industry. This is about finding the ideal companies with the understanding that if you can make a list of 10 companies, at least a few of them will statistically have an opening (or can create one for the right person).

Now, expand the search. If you have historically worked in one industry, finding companies in that space is relatively easy. You obviously know the industry; so make a second list of the companies and individuals in your industry vertical that you need to target. (Some of these might be part of your top 10 list mentioned earlier.)

One thing you may want to consider is to do a Google search for fastest growing companies in your industry. Also be sure to check out the Forbes Top 100 Fastest Growing Companies and the INC 5000. While the Forbes list is better known, the INC 5000 is a list of the top 5000 fastest growing privately held companies. It is a perfect reference for the executive job seeker.

To achieve success faster, it is key to identify your transferable skills and use them to develop a value proposition that will apply not only to the competitors in your industry vertical, but also to other industries where you may have interest and where your role and skill set would function similarly.

Too often people think they are stuck in a specific industry vertical, when in reality it is fairly straightforward to make a leap to another. Branching out to other industries is often very effective—and for the majority of executives reading this book, your "why" has much more to do with people than the product, widget, or service you have been representing in whatever industry you work.

Great companies and leaders seek to add talent who can offer diversity of experience. Use this as leverage and create talking points around it to your advantage. Explain how your experiences are transferable and can provide new ideas and creative solutions.

You can work for any company or industry you want if your value proposition is in alignment with what they seek. However, in order to do this successfully, anybody and everybody who knows your name needs to know your product: the what, the how, and most importantly, the why!

I have found that this process is actually one of the main challenge points for job seeking executives. The process of identifying companies, expanding that search to identify a "similar audience" (pardon the marketing term), and then targeting key decision makers at each organization is key to cold market success. However, it is a skillset that most haven't developed. In addition, without the right software it can be very time consuming.

That's why one of the most valuable things we do for our clients is to help them expand their "top 10 list" and find all companies that match their parameters. Then our software helps to do a deep dive and obtain contact information for each key executive for the company.

Most people we speak with feel like their biggest challenge is getting in front of the right people. The problem is, they don't know who or where they are. This process eliminates that challenge and gives you a functional working list you can work for your job search. It eliminates the unknown and increases predictability of your results.

And at the end of the day, your ideal company is not going to find you: you are probably going to need to find it. And for that, you need to call on your biggest career resource: the power of your network.

YOUR SEARCH BEGINS WITH YOUR NETWORK

It makes sense when you think about it. The most challenging component of building a relationship with the right person is the initial contact and building trust so they have emotional buy in to you. That's why your network is far and away the fastest and most effective place to begin.

There is a common phrase going around the internet these days, "your network is your net worth". That is right on the money when it comes to your career. Not only should you begin your search within your personal network, but once you land your position, you should remain active with your network and cultivate relationships continuously. Afterall, this next position is not likely to be your last. And the stronger your brand is inside of your network, the less likely you will be concerned about where you next job will be.

For now, however, you have an immediate need. Find your ideal position in the fastest time possible. With that need in mind, you need to begin with your current network. There are a couple reasons for this:

1. It is easier to strike up a conversation with them because you have direct access. They will respond to your email or take your phone call. You have name recognition.

2. You already have a relationship. They know your brand already. You might need to articulate more clearly for them, but they already know, like and trust you—and that is the most important thing.

Unfortunately, too many executives shy away from their personal networks. It is not the norm to reach out to friends and colleagues and make them aware of their career situation. I get it...it can be hard. You are probably used to being the one that your network comes to for help, not the one reaching out for help. It will require a bit of vulnerability, but when done properly it will not show desperation.

> **Here is the bottom line, you never know who can network you into the right position. Just because someone in your network doesn't have an executive position with the ability to offer you job, doesn't mean they don't know someone who could. You are always looking to connect with the 2nd and 3rd level of your network - statistics indicate that this where your next job is located.**

> We have even seen a person land a VP position through his dry cleaner. When the dry cleaner found out this gentleman was out of work, he asked what kind of role and company he was seeking. Upon further conversation, the dry cleaner connected his two clients and a VP job was created. The moral of the story: don't judge who may or may not be able to help you.

The reality is, not communicating with your complete network (EVERYONE who knows you), or convincing yourself that you have no network will cost you opportunity, time, and thousands of dollars in lost income. Plus, you will be stuck competing for the 10 to 30% of executive positions that are advertised making your search much more competitive.

It's important to understand that reaching out to your personal network is not begging for a job or an introduction. Money follows value. Your job is to connect with people in your network, ask what's new and important to them, and campaign by sharing your value proposition. If they are going to vote for you (connect you with other people/opportunity), they need to know you are running for office (looking for a job).

People are typically blind to the effectiveness of their own network. While virtually everyone knows that it's not what you know but who you know that will make the difference in you finding your next position, most executives are unable to clearly identify and leverage their own networks.

Indeed, statistics say that networks are where your next job is coming from. Remember, 70 to 90% of executive jobs are never advertised, and according to LinkedIn's research, the #1 way people find a position is through a referral of some kind (via an employee or professional associate).[9] The ONLY way you will hear about these "hidden" jobs is through your network or the networks of your friends and associates.

What's more, your chances of getting to decision-makers is much higher when they get to know you via a "warm" introduction from someone they know who is in your network, rather than a cold call or emailed résumé and cover letter. And since most people like being able to help people they know, like and trust, with the right approach the members of your network should be happy to make connections for you.

---

[9] LinkedIn Talent Solutions, The Ultimate List of Hiring Statistics for Hiring Managers, HR Professionals, and Recruiters, 2015, Ultimate-List-of-Hiring-Stats-v02.04 LinkedIn.pdf, https://business.linkedin.com/content/dam/business/talent-solutions/global/en_us/c/pdfs/Ultimate-List-of-Hiring-Stats-v02.04.pdf

Bottom line: Everyone has a network, but if you feel that you don't have a strong personal network, it is a top priority to build and cultivate your network, starting NOW.

HOW TO DISCOVER OPPORTUNITY AND CONNECT WITH KEY DECISION MAKERS

Now that we have covered cold and warm markets, I want to take a step back and look at your search from a 30,000 foot view. Remember, this isn't always clean. Lines get blurred together. This conversation about networking is not an either / or conversation, but an "and" conversation.

You have to work your warm market, of course. However, the goal of the cold market is not necessarily to land a job. If you did that, you would be navigating your search like most others who are struggling. Instead, your job is to elevate the relationship from them being in your cold market, to being in your warm market. I know that may sound like it will take a lot of time, but I assure you it is the fastest way to get results from your cold market.

Remember, your search can never be about you getting a job, but focusing on them and their problems. Everyone has them. Your job is to identify the problems and/or opportunities, and be able to articulate your unique value proposition and solution(s). Handle it more as a consultant than a job seeker.

In summary, follow this process:

> 1. Start by making a list of the top 10 companies you would be EXCITED to work with. Don't worry about available positions. Just think about the 10 companies you feel you would be able to add great value and would be excited to work with IF there was something available. This will allow you to build a profile for your ideal company.
>
> 2. Expand that list. Do research to find all companies that you don't know about. This can be done with extensive LinkedIn and Google searches using the proper keywords and industry phrases. However, the easiest way is to use their company code with the IRS. You will find that if you make a list of 10 companies, most of them will share the same industry code with the IRS. That's why we use software to build out that list and find every company in the same or similar category. It's an invaluable tool.

3. Build a working list of 20 companies (you can't work more than 20 effectively at a time). As you exhaust efforts on a company, replace it with the next company from your master list.

4. Connect with key decision makers at each company. Once again, you can spend time researching each company to find key decision makers. It is certainly worth the effort, but it is time consuming. That's why with our software, we not only give our clients company names, but also the names and contact information for key decision makers inside of each company.

It's that simple. If you are someone who feels like you can make a massive impact at an organization, but your biggest challenge is knowing which companies to target or how to get in touch with key people inside those organizations, this is the simple, predictable process to target them.

Now that you have the companies and key decision makers in your cross-hairs, it's time to reach out, connect, and cultivate relationships with them. Help bring them from the cold market into your warm market.

STEP 4: CONNECTING AND CULTIVATING RELATIONSHIPS WITH KEY DECISION MAKERS

This chapter is dedicated to teaching you how to engage with individuals who can introduce you to opportunity or create an opportunity for you. Companies are in a constant state of change and there is always some sort of strategic initiative in development. These roles require exceptional talent and this is exactly why you should not be overly focused on only the current openings they may have available.

Getting in front of employers you have identified is more of an art than a science. The process we help our clients go through creates a framework with which you can successfully stand out from the crowd. Rather than showing up with a "Here I am—hire me" mindset, we teach you how to Be Known, Be Liked, Build Trust and Get Hired. This will not only increase your success with your warm network, but it will create a predictable process of expanding your warm network through a networking campaign to your cold network.

One of the most important abilities for any leader is their ability to influence others. We talked earlier in the book about the importance of psychology—specifically, your psychology and mindset with your job search. However, equally important is the psychology of the person looking to hire you or connect you (i.e., influencers, or people who will share your message with others).

To get in front of the decision makers who have the power to offer you the position you want, you need to (1) know who they are, and (2) connect with them personally.

Earlier we talked about the importance of networking and research in developing your marketing package. Let's put both of those two skills into the context of reaching the key players in your job search.

NETWORK YOUR WAY TO DECISION MAKERS BY DEVELOPING RELATIONSHIPS WITH INFLUENCERS IN YOUR FIELD

Influencers are people who have the ability to connect you to other opportunities. They are generally thought leaders who play large roles in their field of expertise. They might also be people who run events or are connected with the Chamber of Commerce or another type of business organization. Or maybe it is a contact on your working list of companies, which is a completely cold contact and you are trying to create a new relationship.

Either way, your job is to develop a relationship with them. It is key to acknowledge their success and ask for their help and advice. Influencers are typically people who like to help others, so acknowledging their place and success in the market, and telling them you value their opinion and advice will go a long way.

Be sure to offer your help to them in turn. Invest time and energy into learning about them and see how you can add value to them. Maybe you can connect them with someone in your network. Maybe you can help them in a consultative nature the way you would help a business. You are not selling yourself directly, but in a roundabout way by helping to solve problems for other people.

Remember, people work with people they know, like and trust—and sometimes the trust part of the equation takes time. Besides, you are not typically talking to the decision maker when you are talking to an influencer, so just focus on building rapport, interest in what you do, and make sure your message is remembered.

Be patient and focus on cultivating the relationship—it will be worth it when you are able to ask the influencer to provide you with an introduction to the decision maker you want to reach.

FIND THE DECISION MAKERS BY STARTING AT THE TOP OF YOUR TARGETED COMPANIES

Throughout this book we've talked about finding companies you'd like to work for and then researching their mission statement and focus to make sure it's a good fit for you. Once you've done that, you're ready to reach out to the decision makers via your connections.

The key to success is to start as high in the organization as possible. Strangely, these people are typically easier to find because they are the "front-facing" personalities of the organization. Once you identify them, you can tailor your marketing plan for them and then create a strategy to reach them directly.

Make sure you figure out their needs and focus on adding value as this will help you stand out. While this method is not guaranteed to succeed, it will certainly increase the probability of them meeting with you, even if they are not currently hiring for a specific position.

Remember the importance of psychology, both yours and theirs. Your job is to get into their head and heart to figure out what's important to them and you'll know how to position your value proposition so it resonates. This is not about you needing a job. This is about you connecting with the executive and delivering a message that connects with them based on their needs.

Now that you know who you are going to be reaching out to, let's talk about how you can reach them most effectively.

THE PROS AND CONS OF DIFFERENT MODES OF COMMUNICATION TO REACH DECISION MAKERS

No matter what actions you are taking as part of your job search, you must remember that you are dealing with humans with all sorts of personality types and preferences. Your job is to use all the different modes of communication systematically with each person until you have success.

Remember, this isn't about you, it is about them; so suit your communication to their preference, not yours. For instance, if you wanted to reach Mary, the CEO, and your preferred method of communication is email, but she prefers phone calls, sending her a bunch of emails won't be effective. Even if the phone makes you nervous, you'd better be prepared to get your courage up and dial.

All of the different modes of communication have their pluses and minuses. Let's go through them and discuss how you can use each one effectively.

#1: Email

Pros:

- *Fast and efficient.*
- *Excellent to use with those with whom you have an established relationship.*
- *Easy to include attachments (your marketing package if applicable).*
- *Convenient to access on all of your devices.*

Cons:

- *Overused by most job seekers so it can seem "spammy"—it's hard to stand out with an email.*
- *Need to be very creative in your writing to get noticed.*
- *Chance they never see your email based on their filters (spam box).*
- *Easy for them to delete quickly, along with the hundreds of other emails they delete every day.*
- *Your attachments may not be opened out of fear of downloading a virus.*

If you are sending an email, pay particular attention to the subject line, as this will often make the difference between having your email opened or deleted. Assuming you are emailing someone you know, put your name in the subject line ("From Joe Smith") in case they don't recognize your email address. Then indicate clearly what you want to communicate.

As an example, "From Joe Smith: The materials we spoke about," or "From Joe Smith: Following up from our conversation of X-date" (the last time you contacted them). Make sure that the subject line reminds them of your connection with them. That way the email will be less likely to end up in spam.

If you are emailing someone you don't know personally but who is connected to a member of your network, you MUST put that network member's name in the subject line: "From Joe Smith—Sue Simons recommended I connect with you." Again, including the name of someone this individual should know in the subject line makes it more likely the email will be opened.

We also recommend not attaching any documents to the initial email to prevent it from ending up in spam. Make the offer to send them your marketing package once they reply to you—at that point you should be included on their "safe contacts" list and any documents you send will go through.

#2: PHONE CALL

Pros:

- *Easy to make a call.*
- *Great way to develop a relationship. More personal than email.*
- *Less people are making phone calls these days—you will stand out a little more.*

Cons:

- *Can be challenging to get by gatekeepers whose job is to keep you from getting through.*
- *Easy to miss a call, forcing you to leave a voicemail and play phone tag, dragging out the process.*

It is ESSENTIAL that whenever possible you get the executive's direct phone line rather than going through the receptionist, switchboard or automated greeting. You might have to make an initial phone call to get the direct number, or ask if your network connection can give it to you.

Sometimes the most effective way to reach a decision maker is to call before and after regular business hours. Most executives tend to arrive earlier and stay later than their support staff (or "gatekeepers") so you might be more likely to reach the executive directly.

Especially for the initial phone call, persist until you actually speak to the executive. Leaving a message with the gatekeeper or (worse) a voicemail is a recipe for failure.

If you do end up with the gatekeeper, be very pleasant. Some of our clients have developed great relationships with the gatekeepers first. Then, when it was time to ask to be put through to the decision maker, the gatekeeper was more likely to do so.

In the best of all possible worlds, the network connection who knows the decision maker will have already called or emailed to introduce you. That way, when you call, the first thing you should do is to mention the name of your connection. This will refresh the decision maker's memory and usually will make him or her more receptive to your call.

#3: SENDING A LETTER

Pros:

- While letters used to be a staple, few people use them effectively anymore. When done right, it is easier to reach the decision maker and stand out.
- Anytime you handwrite the address on the envelope, open rates will go up.
- Increased likelihood of reaching the decision maker. Hint: Increase your odds by marking it "Private & Confidential."

Cons:

- Delivery takes time.
- You won't know if they received it unless you pay for delivery confirmation.
- Writing, packing, and mailing the letter takes more time than an email or social media message (like LinkedIn).

We have had many clients who have written a masterful letter and delivered it via U.S. mail directly to the CEO. This is always the best way to go, because the CEO often has people around him/her who are trained to speak with you, to welcome you with open arms. These people are the face of the company. Therefore, when you go to the CEO's office with any correspondence, the treatment is precisely the antithesis of what you will experience in the HR department.

When you go directly to a CEO, you will be able to speak with real people. Even if they don't give your letter to the CEO, you can be sure that wherever it goes, it will receive top-tier attention.

A client, George, sent a strategically positioned letter directly to Bruce, the CEO of a large manufacturing company. When we followed up on the letter, Bruce's secretary answered the phone. After we talked with her for a few minutes, she put us through directly to Bruce. That led to an interview with two different people in the company, which then led to two separate job offers for George—and they let him choose which position he wanted!

#4: SOCIAL MEDIA

Pros:

- Very easy and efficient.
- Easy to reach decision makers.
- The receiver of the message is likely to check out your profile. If you use LinkedIn, that essentially means they will look at your marketing package.
- Often the recipient will be notified of your message in multiple locations, increasing the odds of them reading it.

Cons:

- Most platforms don't allow attachments (not an issue with LinkedIn).
- Character limits to share your message (not an issue with LinkedIn).
- You may need a premium account to be completely effective with your strategy, so there is a cost.

Assuming you have a premium LinkedIn account, you can send what are called InMail messages to people who are not your first-degree connections (they are connected with people you know but you are not connected with them yet). Or, if a decision maker is part of the same LinkedIn Group as you, you can send them a message directly or through the Group.

As said above, the great thing about connecting via LinkedIn is that the decision maker can instantly see your profile and any materials you post on it. It is a quick way for them to get to know you and what you have to offer.

#5: FACE TO FACE

Pros:
- *Instantaneous results: an interview on the spot.*
- *You stand out from the competition—very few have the confidence to start with face to face.*

Cons:
- *The only "con" is self-imposed. Face to face requires you having the confidence and preparation to show up to the right event, the right recruiter, or the right employer unannounced.*
- *Can be a lot of wasted time if you don't handle it correctly.*

Again, remember that most executives are busy people, so showing up unannounced at their office might backfire. However, if your network connection sets up a meeting for you (and perhaps accompanies you), AND you are confident enough to put yourself on the line, a face-to-face meeting can reap large rewards.

A somewhat lower risk approach might be for your network connection to arrange for lunch or cocktails for you, your connection, and the decision maker. Meeting outside the office and in a more social setting is often easier and puts less pressure on all parties concerned.

A third option is to discover if the decision maker will be attending any kind of professional conference, meeting, networking gathering, etc. At these occasions it's very normal to meet and speak with new people with whom you know you have something in common.

To make the most of such an encounter, make sure you have your elevator speech ready to go—but NEVER start with it. Instead, ask questions of the decision maker and discover more about him or her first. After a few minutes of this, most people will reciprocate and ask you about yourself. Only then can you talk about who you are, what you're passionate about, and your expertise.

IMPORTANT NOTE: These kinds of social occasions are not the place to ask for a job. They are occasions for you to begin developing a relationship with decision makers so you can follow up at a later point and explore possible executive opportunities. This is part of the "Be Known, Be Liked, Build Trust and Get Hired" strategy.

And remember, your confidence and mindset with this process is of vital importance. Have fun with this. Approach it as a game. Test different methods, with different people, in a different order. You might find you are getting better results with one method over another. It is truly a trial and error proposal.

A final reminder: Don't use all of these communication avenues at the same time—you don't want the person you are trying to reach to feel bombarded. But DO make sure that (1) you're matching the other person's preferred communication strategy, especially and first, and (2) you create and follow a systematic plan for keeping in touch after the initial contact.

THE 3 P'S X 2: PACKAGE, POSITION, PROMOTE AND PREPARE, BE PROACTIVE, PERSIST

It is all about the follow up. The likelihood of you getting through on your first attempt is slim to none. Think about it: you are trying to contact a busy executive. If you are going to succeed, you are going to have to master the follow up, and that simply takes practice.

We organize the key principles of your job search into two sets of three P's. The first set is **Package, Position and Promote**. We've covered all three pretty thoroughly in this book, but it is important you do them in the right order, i.e., you'd better have yourself packaged and positioned in the marketplace properly before you run out promoting and selling yourself.

The old idea of "ready, fire, aim" that may have made you fairly successful in your business likely won't work in your executive search. That's why we always start with the marketing and branding (packaging and positioning). Only once we know the story do we promote (i.e., sell). Taking any other method will be professional suicide.

The second of our three P's is to Prepare, be Proactive and Persist. These deal more with your psychology than anything else.

1. Prepare

Preparation has two connotations. As we've said before, the human race is capable of emotionally dealing with anything we are prepared for. It is the things we are not prepared for that throw us off our game. So be sure to have a clear understanding of your environment and mentally prepare as much as possible for all outcomes.

The second part of preparation is straightforward. Your ability to land your dream position is predicated on your ability to effectively communicate your value proposition to the right people. There is no "three strikes and you're out rule" in your executive search. You get one pitch, and it's either a hit or a strikeout. Hopefully, it's a home run.

Preparation for each conversation is essential for success. Don't just wing it. Do your research. Figure out their needs. What holes can you plug? What problems can your skill set solve? Prepare properly, then go into the conversation and ask very strategic, pointed questions. You will find you talk far less, but your words go much farther. We'll talk extensively about the executive interview in the next chapter.

2. Be Proactive

Every executive we have ever spoken to understands that in order to be successful in business, you need to have a proactive strategy. If you are running a business and you become reactive in any market, you are in big trouble.

That said, virtually every executive we speak with takes a very reactive approach trying to find their next position when they are out of work. They create a résumé, blast it out, maybe share it with some key contacts, maybe connect with a few recruiters...and wait.

Is that what you would do with your business? If your business lost a main source of revenue and was struggling to get by, would you simply blast some information out, make a couple of perceived key connections (recruiters), and wait for your phone to ring? NO WAY!

You would figure out what went wrong, develop a strategy to fix it, find the resources you need to fill the gap and work tirelessly until you fixed the problem. That is exactly what you need to do with your executive job search.

We say that we help our clients find their ideal executive position 400% faster than the industry average because it proves the importance of the kind of proactive approach we take with each of our clients. Whether you work with an executive search consultant or not, you must put 100% of your energy into getting stuff done and moving the needle NOW.

3. Persist

Your executive job search is not going to be all roses and sunshine. It is going to be hard. It will test you psychologically. It will make you question yourself. That is where the importance of the process and personal coaching can provide immense value. When you have faith in the process, you have faith in achieving a positive result of finding the position you seek. Accompanied with personal coaching, it can make the experience a lot easier, enable you to keep your head down, trudge along and be persistent until you realize success.

COMMUNICATING WITH AN EXECUTIVE RECRUITER

For many executive candidates, the first step to reaching a decision maker and getting a job interview is the recruiter. And they often decide whether your résumé lands on a hiring manager's desk or in the nearest recycling bin.

While it's important to know the basics of what recruiters do, you also need to know what they DON'T do. After all, you don't want an inappropriate request to ruin your chances for an interview.

Here are four things you shouldn't ask of a recruiter.

#1: Don't be overly friendly.
Recruiters are people. They are normally going to be warm, friendly, and helpful. After all, it's their job to guide you through the hiring process. But remember, they are not professional colleagues. It's important that you never forget that.

Treat the recruiter as a respected coworker. It's good to be friendly, but don't be overly casual. It's usually good practice to keep personal conversations, jokes and physical contact to a minimum.

A HELPFUL RULE OF THUMB IS: DON'T SAY OR DO ANYTHING IN FRONT OF A RECRUITER THAT YOU WOULDN'T SAY OR DO IN FRONT OF YOUR BOSS.

#2: Don't expect career coaching.
The recruiter's goal is not to help you get a job: it's to help you navigate the hiring process at one specific company. Recruiters aren't career coaches, so don't ask them to help you craft your cover letter, edit your résumé or plan your career path. That's simply not what they do.

You can ask questions about the company or industry in general, but try to relate your questions to the job you're being considered for. And save your best, most thoughtful questions for the hiring manager or decision maker—that's who you need to impress.

#3: Don't ask for insider information.

There's only one job candidate you really need to worry about: you. It may be tempting, but don't ask about who you're up against for a job. Recruiters are unlikely to share any information about other candidates, anyways. All you will accomplish by asking is making yourself seem insecure about your own abilities and qualifications.

You can, however, ask questions about the hiring process and the position itself. **Here are a few questions you can feel comfortable asking:**

- *Are you still interviewing candidates?*
- *How large is the current pool of candidates?*
- *How would you describe the ideal candidate for the job?*
- *Is there anything I can do to make myself a stronger candidate?*

BOTTOM LINE, THE BEST WAY TO GET AN EDGE ON THE COMPETITION IS TO MAKE YOURSELF A MORE COMPETITIVE CANDIDATE.

#4: Don't request special treatment.

Here is the reality, you are not the only candidate for the position. The recruiters alliance and allegiance is not with you, it is with the company. While recruiters are often happy to help, understand that they are never helping with the aim of advocating for you. They are doing what they need to fill a position.

It is never helpful to ask a recruiter to put in a good word with the decision maker - it will only cause damage in your hiring process. Trust me, if they think you are the best candidate, they will naturally put in a good word for you. That's their job.

In addition, don't ask them to relay any messages to the decision maker for you. Instead, send a note or take the initiative to communicate directly. That will highlight your confidence and give an opportunity for one more chance to stand out.

THREE REASONS WHY A RECRUITER OR NETWORK CONTACT IS NOT CALLING YOU BACK

Have you ever spoken with another executive in your network or a recruiter who has promised to share your resume with his/her network - only to have two weeks go by with no action, no results, and to make matters worse your contact has vanished?

You call them, leave messages, but it's crickets... You're probably frustrated and wondering what went wrong.

There are some common mistakes people make, and chances are that if you have or are experiencing this, you have made a couple of them.

MISTAKE #1: YOU MADE IT ALL ABOUT YOU.

It's human nature. We are all inherently selfish to a certain extent. Did you take the time to ask how things were going in his/her career? Are they looking for something bigger and better? Did you start by trying to figure out how you can add value into his/her life or career?

One of my first mentors used to say, "you have two ears and one mouth, use them accordingly". That means, two-thirds of the conversation should be focused on you asking questions about them and seeing how you can serve them. If you do that, trust me, you will have an opportunity the last one-third of the conversation to make your targeted ask for help. It just can't be all about you and your needs.

MISTAKE #2: NO ACCOUNTABILITY OR CALL TO ACTION.

This is a two way street. It is always an exchange of value. There needs to be a clear call to action with deadlines and accountability. Before you finish your conversation, make sure you do these three things:

Be 100% clear on what you can do for them
Make a clear call to action on how they can help you
Schedule a time to follow up. If it isn't on the calendar, it isn't real.

The fact that you are leading with adding value to them will increase your odds of not being blown off. In addition, by you helping them, they will feel obligated to help you. One little piece of advice: make sure you don't give them everything you have until they have fulfilled their end of the deal. That will keep them fully engaged with assisting you!

MISTAKE #3: YOU APPEAR NEEDY OR AS IF YOU'RE SELLING SOMETHING

Remember who you are. You are a solution provider and a problem solver! If people don't see the value in connecting with you or are not respecting your time, then move on. And, you are not trying to connect with everyone, only the right people. You want to stay professionally engaged, but never come off as needy or salesy. That just screams of desperation...and the one thing no executive can sell is desperation!

When I speak with somebody in my network on your behalf, here's a version of what I might say:

"I have a senior executive in my network I would love to connect you with. After review of their background, it looks like there could be some great synergies. They are in the market right now, but I am certain s/he will land a new role soon, and when s/he does, the chance to get him/her will be gone. Let me know and I would be happy to put you in touch."

We are all human and make mistakes. I find that people are typically willing to give you a second chance if you have made any or all of these mistakes. All you need to do is give them a call and start the conversation over.

If they decide to not give you a second chance, chalk it up as a learning experience and count it as one of the many no's you will endure during your search…then move on.

GO FOR NO

This is probably one of the most challenging psychological elements of your search. The fear of rejection can be paralyzing. This comes back to one of my favorite statements, "we can deal with anything we expect".

This is sales 101. Your job search is a numbers game. Sure, you want to connect and cultivate relationships with as many key individuals as possible, but you also need to be realistic about expectations. Remember, you are reaching out to a cold market. They have no emotional connection to you and are likely very busy.

Sometimes they mean "know" (meaning they want to know more about you. This is essentially a "maybe"), and sometimes they actually mean "NO." Either way, it is fine. In fact, it's great. You are not trying to connect with everyone - only the right people. The faster you get to NO, the quicker you will know where to spend your time actually cultivating the relationships.

Point of caution, don't get caught up in the "maybe" zone. Try to seek clarity from your contact and ascend them from maybe to NO or, even better, YES!

But once again, it is all about expectations and numbers. Like all sales jobs, you will hear NO far more than yes. In fact, often times, this is what it looks like:

NO NO NO NO NO NO NO NO NO NO NO NO NO NO NO NO NO NO NO NO NO NO NO NO NO NO NO NO NO NO NO NO NO NO NO NO NO NO NO NO NO NO NO NO NO NO NO NO NO NO NO NO NO NO NO NO NO NO NO NO NO NO NO NO NO… YES!

You see, every NO got you closer to a YES. Don't shy away from the NO - embrace it. Don't take on the negative energy that comes with the NO - realize that they are not rejecting you, they probably have something else going on and you are simply not a priority for them. That is completely normal. You have probably done it yourself at one point or another.

Either way, there is no place in your search for MAYBE. If you have anyone that falls into that category, muster up the courage to give them a call and move them into either the NO or YES category. Then you will know with who you should be spending your precious time cultivating relationships.

Once you've reached a decision maker and they are interested in you, the next critical step is the executive interview. While there are many pitfalls to be avoided during the interview, there are some clear and simple strategies you can use to move on to the job offer. The next chapter will help you ace your next interview.

HOW TO NAVIGATE THE INTERVIEW

05

How to Navigate the Interview

Congratulations!

You have made it to the next step in your job search. The company/employer/decision maker has asked you to come in for an interview. They have decided to spend and invest their time with you. They are not trying to trick you: they are trying to learn more about you. They want you to demonstrate your skills in the areas where you can make the greatest impact in the company.

These types of interviews happen very rarely at this level, so the interviewers are likely not that experienced (although they may believe they are). So with proper preparation, you can help to guide the interview.

> **Remember, in the interview, you have as much *power* as they do.**

They need someone to fill an important position, so don't go into the interview feeling like you need them and they don't need you. Think of yourself as the seller of a valuable commodity rather than someone asking for a job. You should be interviewing them as much as they are interviewing you, to see if the opportunity is the right fit for you.

THE CONFIDENCE/COMPETENCE LOOP

Confidence is ultimately the key to your success in any interview. And **preparation** builds confidence in the message you are looking to communicate. The more you prepare, the more competent you are, and the more confidence you will have. That confidence/competence loop continues into infinity.

I ALWAYS SAY THAT THE INTERVIEW IS WON DURING PREPARATION BECAUSE **THAT IS WHEN YOU WILL ULTIMATELY DISCOVER YOUR TRUE VALUE**.

When you have a clear understanding of the message you are communicating about your value proposition to the company, it gives you the power to influence the direction of the interview. This way you don't feel like you are going into the interview to face a "firing squad" of questions. Instead, you will go in with a message you know is going to resonate with the interviewer—allowing you to create a two-way dialogue.

I always say that the interview is won during preparation because that is when you will ultimately discover your true value. That's why we use the EPIC system (I'll talk about that soon) to prepare for every executive interview. Your goal is to gather as much data as possible and build the relevant bridges showing you as the best fit for the organization with who you are interviewing.

We talk a lot about the need for you to interview them as much as they are interviewing you. If you do the EPIC system, it will help you build your competence around where the company is, where they are looking to go, and how you can position yourself as the best fit. That will, in turn, give you the confidence to stand out as the best candidate for the job.

Remember, it isn't the best candidate that gets the job, but the best prepared candidate that gets the job. So make sure you put time into your preparation.

WE ALL MAKE DECISIONS EMOTIONALLY

We like to think we are far more sophisticated, but we all make emotional decisions. The house you bought, the car you drive, the college you attended…all based upon emotion rather than reason or logic, right?

The good news for you is that the individuals interviewing you are about to make an emotional decision about you. Executives typically pride themselves on their intuition. They trust their gut feelings, if you will.

This means their decision about you is not entirely based on intellect and you've probably heard the expression, "people buy on emotion, then justify with logic."

"Do you 'feel' like the right candidate for the job?" That's what they will be thinking. That's why your only job in the interview is to make sure you are prepared enough to influence their intuition in your favor.

HOW TO PREPARE FOR THE INTERVIEW USING OUR EPIC™ SYSTEM

So, how do you prepare for the interview? What do you focus on, and in what order, to have an effective game plan that will guarantee a positive result?

In his book, Start With Why: How Great Leaders Inspire Everyone to Take Action, Simon Sinek speaks of the golden circle and the importance of knowing your why. Using his metaphor, we have created the "golden" Executive Preparation for Interviews Circle (EPIC™). And just like Sinek's golden circle, the closer you can get to the core of the circle, the more effective you will be.

There are five levels for our Executive Preparation for Interview Circle (EPIC). The more you research and understand each level, the more prepared you will be to ace the interview.

NOTE: NEVER accept a last-minute interview. You need at least five solid days of preparation time for the interview to be effective.

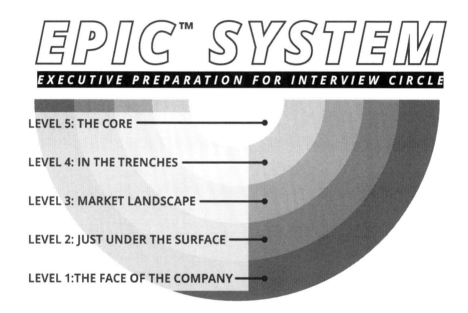

Let's go through each level.

LEVEL 1: THE FACE OF THE COMPANY.

Level 1 is the organization's website and social media. Most people get through Level 1 of a company's value ladder relatively successfully. However, when you are checking the website, be sure not to stop on the "About Us" page.

Check out any media tabs; get up to date on any current happenings in the news you need to understand. Dig as deep into the website as possible to find out as much as you can.

Websites are easy to explore because they are normally pretty static—they don't update too often. However, if you really want your finger on the pulse of the company, make sure to check their social media presence as well. Information on social media is available almost immediately, so it is essential to tune in to everything happening on places like LinkedIn, Facebook and Instagram.

Pay particular attention to, and make notes about the company's challenges and opportunities. These are the key areas you should weave into your presentation. It's especially effective in the interview to show how your value proposition can help them solve problems and create opportunities.

An important point that is very basic but worth mentioning. You must make it very clear how your CV/résumé matches up with the job description of the position you're being considered for. Make sure to spend some time building five or more "bridges" from your skills and experiences, showing how they will fill the responsibilities and needs of your desired role.

LEVEL 2: JUST UNDER THE SURFACE.

The next level is a deeper dive into the entire company. You are looking for information that is publicly available but may require a bit more effort to dig up.

One of the great tools you can leverage for this is Google Alerts. All you need to do is type "Google Alerts" into Google and enter the name of the company. You will then be updated anytime Google picks up any new information on that company. It's a very valuable tool.

To set up your Google alerts go to www.Google.com/alerts. It is very simple.

Make sure to do a deep dive into the finances of the company. Even if it isn't completely relevant for your position or role, knowing the current state of the company's finances and any recent financial trends can give you key information on past performance as well as the current trajectory of the organization.

Another great practice is to get as much company literature as you can. Call the marketing department and ask them to send you available information. If they ask who you are, tell them. Let them know you are preparing to interview for a position, and name the person interviewing you. Chances are the marketing department will relay information about your request to the person interviewing you, which will show your thorough preparation.

Finally, find the profiles for each person interviewing you. Look on the company website and on LinkedIn. You want not just professional information but also hobbies, family, etc. What makes them tick? Where can you find commonality?

Another benefit to LinkedIn: when you look at someone's profile, it will alert them that you looked, which will often prompt the person to spend time looking at your information. Providing you have followed our advice earlier in the book about optimizing your LinkedIn profile, the more time they spend on your profile, the better!

You also can use the interviewer's LinkedIn profile to check for contacts you have in common. You can use those names as a great icebreaker at the start of the interview.

If you have a strong relationship with any of connections you and the interviewer share, be sure to call that individual and ask for information. You sometimes can get very valuable "intelligence" using this strategy.

The call will go something like this:

"Hey Matt, it's Chris Kirkpatrick. How are you? The reason for my call is that I am in the final stages of a confidential interview process for an executive position, and I noticed that we are both connected with the person who is interviewing me. I was wondering what your relationship with him/her was, and if there was anything you could let me know about him/her?"

If there is not a strong relationship, don't bring it up. But if there is a strong relationship with this shared connection, it can be a great way for you to start the conversation. You can tell the interviewer that you noticed you had a shared connection in John and that you spoke with him about the position (if that doesn't break confidentiality). It will be another layer of influence and more social proof for you.

LEVEL 3: MARKET LANDSCAPE.

As you dive deeper into the core of the business, it is important to have a deeper understanding of the industry and market conditions as well. Do research on industry-specific websites and/or publications. (Google Alerts is also a great tool for this).

Remember, in order for you to stand apart from the competition, it is important for you to be as well rounded and well versed in their business as you can. This will allow you to demonstrate in the interview your expertise and understanding of their industry and the market conditions they are facing. This is another great way to demonstrate how you can fix challenges or create opportunities that are directly related to their business.

LEVEL 4: IN THE TRENCHES.

If you really want to understand how a business is running at ground level, you need to visit it. Your objective is to experience the company on as deep a level as possible. It will give you amazing insight and great ideas.

There are a lot of opportunities to access a company you are interviewing with. If it has any sort of consumer-facing locations (such as a retail store or outlet), go visit. Don't try to be covert about it either: talk to the employees and ask them as many questions as you can. Talk to the manager and let them know you are interviewing with the company (you don't need to be specific about the position you are interviewing for). Tell them you are seeking insights about what the company is like at ground level.

If the company doesn't have any physical locations, it is likely they will still have an opportunity for you to experience their product or service process online. Who are their customers and suppliers? Dig as deep into this information as you can.

Do what a typical client would do so you can get the same ground level experience. See where their processes are working and where they might need to improve (and how you can help them do it). You will be amazed with what you can come away with that can make a massive impact on the interview.

Remember, you are applying for a leadership position, so you should think of the interview more as a consultation than an interviewee. This one strategy will set you miles apart from most of the competition.

LEVEL 5: THE CORE.

If you have handled Levels 1 through 4 effectively, you will have many keen insights that have helped you drill down to the core of the business. You should be able to succinctly break down all of the information you have gathered and summarized for the individual or panel what is going on in the organization at a high level.

It is also important to know where the interviewer stands on these matters so you form your summary accordingly. What is important to them? Use the information you gathered from reading their profiles or talking with their connections to figure this out.

men, come to the interview with a launch plan". essentially a mini business plan for what you will do in your first 90 days with the company. (One of the things we do with our clients is to teach them how to put their launch plan together effectively.)

Remember, the company has likely already spent a lot of time, money and resources on searching for the right candidate. Your ability to convey to them that you are willing, able and excited to hit the ground running will often play largely into their decision.

BEFORE THE INTERVIEW: YOUR APPEARANCE CHECKLIST

The next time you are in the supermarket, go to the back of the store to where the day-old baked goods and other less desirable merchandise is kept. You'll likely see a shelf of dented cans of vegetables and fruit. Come back two weeks later and we guarantee that those cans will still be there. Why? Nobody wants a dented can!

You want to make sure that the people interviewing you won't perceive you as a "dented can" because of your age or appearance. Remember, you want to be an executive of this company, so you need to look as if you will fit in to their upper management ranks.

Are you in shape? Do you have a firm handshake? How's your smile? How's your energy level? Do you have the proper wardrobe? If it's been a while since you've interviewed, you need to do a head-to-toe check to ensure that your appearance says "top executive."

Here are seven things you can do to avoid the dented can syndrome:

1. Exercise, healthy diet, exercise, healthy diet. If you think you need to lose 20 pounds, lose 30.
2. Remove facial hair. (Has anybody ever told you they weren't hired because they didn't have a beard?) Cut your hair, trim your fingernails, whiten your teeth and straighten your posture.

3. Buy at least one new suit and have it tailored to fit you exactly.

Then use this for your apparel checklist for interview day.

- *Knee-high socks the same color as your trousers*
- *White shirt with cuffs exactly ½ -inch longer than jacket cuffs with your arms extended*
- *Button the little button between your cuff and elbow (every button must be buttoned)*
- *Tie - avoid red ties, blue tends to be the most recommended color, avoid anything too over the top*
- *Tie your tie knot so it is crisp (silk or semi-silk ties are good for this)*
- *No rings other than a wedding ring (if you haven't thrown that college ring away, do so now)*
- *Easy on the cologne (or none)*
- *Black shoes when wearing navy or charcoal, brown shoes if wearing brown, and always perfectly polished*

Ladies, most of you have all of this figured out already. But we do suggest that you wear a suit for all interviews.

4. Make a list of your quantifiable success and executive accomplishments. Read it often, memorize it and recite it backwards and forwards. These accomplishments are confidence-builders and great reminders of the value you bring to the table.

5. Arrive at every interview at least one hour early. Remain in your car as you subliminally get used to your surroundings. Like an actor waiting backstage, rehearse the interview in your mind.

6. **Enter the building 20 minutes early to acclimate to the environment. Then use the restroom and have a final look in the mirror to be sure your product is gleaming.**

7. Smile: it's the best appearance-improver and confidence-builder around!

GREAT QUESTIONS INVITE REVELATION

You never want the interview to be an interrogation. Instead, it needs to be a conversation where you are in control. You want to balance giving information about yourself with finding out about the company and whether this position is a great fit for you. You also want to be seen as the ideal solution for all of their problems. Once you understand that these are the goals of the interview, you can drive the dialogue down any road you want.

Therefore, don't be afraid to flip the questions on the interviewer. Ask them, "What was it in my résumé that you found to be of the most interest?" When they tell you why, you will know precisely what you should start talking about.

> **REMEMBER,**
>
> People don't want a drill because they want a drill: they need a drill because they want a hole. It is the same for you. They have a problem: that is why you are being interviewed. Figure out what that problem is, offer the right solution and you are in!

Usually people show up for an interview, sit down, engage in a little small talk and then wait for the interviewer to start asking questions. That may work at lower levels—but you are not interviewing for a lower level position. The company is bringing you in to drive change in the organization and lead.

Always, always, always...please start the interview by asking these two questions as they will give you tremendous insight on their needs, restrictions and how you should frame your responses:

1. Before we begin, how much time do you have allocated for our conversation today?
2. What's important to you with respect to this role and what information would you like to know about me?

You are not a job candidate. You are here to offer a solution. You are the white knight riding in on his horse with solutions. You are a solution provider.

A solution provider would never sit through an interview for 45-plus minutes and just answer ridiculous questions without ever asking what the company needs. How can they expect you to come in and drive change and lead if you can't lead the interview process? Make sure to create the environment of a dialogue or you have no shot.

The best way to do this is to ask great questions that will drive the subject matter into your area of expertise. Be careful, though: be sure to only ask questions you know the answers to (which won't be too challenging if you used the EPIC process to prepare).

If you do this properly, all they will be hearing and feeling is that you are an expert. At the end of an hour they're going to be like, "Man, this guy knows everything!" Of course you do…you were the one driving the dialogue without them even realizing it.

We call this interview process EPIC training and we train all our clients in it. It gives them the ability to go into any job interview scenario, quickly ascertain pain points and problems, and then articulate effective solutions.

HOW TO ANSWER THE QUESTION "WHAT'S YOUR GREATEST WEAKNESS?"

At one time or another we all have been faced with the dreaded "What's your greatest weakness" question. We dread the question because the interviewer is virtually asking why they shouldn't hire you!

This query has been an enduring weapon in the hiring manager's arsenal, but most people still have trouble with it. Answer too frankly and you'll torpedo your prospects; use a canned answer and you'll seem phony, or worse, evasive.

A savvy interviewer may even disguise the "weakness" question by posing it in a different way. Here are a few examples:

- Tell me about a project that did not work out so well.
- Name three self-limiting thoughts.
- Tell me about a time in your career that you really goofed up.
- What kind of people do you find it difficult to work with?
- What makes you angry?
- How have your weaknesses affected your job performance?

There is no one answer to the "weakness" question. Sure, you can describe a weakness that has nothing to do with the job you are applying for; or you could say, "Uh...chocolate". Please don't say you are a perfectionist or that you work too hard—all these answers are too deflective and will portray you in a bad light.

Also, if they ask what are your greatest weaknesses, only give them one. This is a question you cannot dodge, but no sense making it easy for them to disqualify you. And, it's never a good idea to say something like, "I struggle with being on time for meetings." I don't care what job you're interviewing for, time management is always going to be important.

HOW TO FORMULATE AN ANSWER FOR ANY "WEAKNESS" QUESTION

All interview answers are like all good stories: they must have a happy ending. Here is our formula for answering the weakness question. It's always a good idea to:

1. Put your weaknesses in the past or at least in perspective.
2. Find something that is grounded in truth and provide an example of how you have grown demonstrating your emotional intelligence.

3. Identify what you've learned and end with a positive outcome.
4. Once you've answered, I like to flip the question on the interviewer in a respectful way that encourages them to share which will enhance the connection with you.

Here's a sample response to the question, "what is your greatest weakness?" Response:

"I think it's interesting how we learn to adapt and play to our strengths. I'd have to say that in the past I struggled with patience. As a consistent top-performing sales professional, I expected a great deal from myself and from others around me. I also believe that being a little impatient at times is what fueled my drive and enabled me to be so successful. However, as I've matured into leadership roles, I've learned to be more self-aware, slow down to better appreciate the wins and take responsibility for effective communication to truly understand the needs of the people around me. The $2.2M deal we did with XYZ company last year required me to lead a team of 10 people to work together under tight timelines and it was a significant achievement for our organization. At the end of the day, none of us are perfect and we're all working to improve something. What is it you're working on?"

When done properly, you will demonstrate integrity by not evading the question, and you will end your answer with a powerful and factual outcome based on your ability to successfully convert the weakness to a strength. By flipping the question back to them, you'll also keep the power balance in check.

There is no possible way to prepare and rehearse an individual answer for every potential weakness question. That's why it is important to have a systematic approach on how you think about, formulate, and respond to those questions. Like anything else, this will take practice to seem authentic. Make a list of these questions and practice in front of a camera (use your smartphone).

ADDITIONAL KEY QUESTIONS YOU SHOULD BE PREPARED TO ANSWER

While we cover how to answer and prepare for all of these 10 questions in much more depth inside of our Interview Masterclass, I did want to touch base on the most important questions you need to be prepared to answer. If you want more detailed instructions, check out the Interview Masterclass at www.CareerNextAgency.com.

One thing to keep in mind is that you should be able to answer all of these questions within a few minutes. If your answer starts to extend beyond the two to three minute line, you need to tighten it up.

1. TELL ME ABOUT YOURSELF?

You should be able to answer this question in 1-2 minutes. It's a lazy opening question that interviewers open the interview with, but it is very common. What they really mean is, "tell me why you are a good candidate for this position and why you are interested in our company"

Often times, the interviewee hasn't fully considered what their response will be, but it is the perfect opportunity to control the narrative of the conversation.

You need to consider items about yourself that are relevant to the company, how it relates to organizational success, and what makes you uniquely qualified for the position. This is a chance for you to give a snapshot of how you want them to view you. It's your best opportunity during the entire interview to build your brand.

As a framework to answer this question, it's always good to include the following four criteria in each response:

1. A statement about what you do better than anyone else.
2. Identify your top three abilities as it relates to the company and people you are interviewing with.
3. Your answer needs to be succinct and specific to the company and position.
4. You should have a clear closing statement with why you are a great fit and interested in this opportunity. This statement should be something that shows you have taken the time to do extensive research.

> **REMEMBER,**
> You are a leader and they are looking to bring you in to lead a company. Prove that leadership out of the gate and create a dialogue, not a one-way interview. Finish by asking them a question, such as:

1. Asking about why they were interested in this company.
2. What do they love most about this company?
3. Why were they interested in speaking with you?

It is almost 100% that you will deal with this question at some point near the beginning of the interview process. If you answer with this framework, you will be lightyears ahead of your competition.

2. WHAT'S YOUR MANAGEMENT STYLE?

This question is diving deeper to see if you are the right fit for their company and culture. Use caution and avoid cliche statements like, "I'm a servant leader".

It's really important to understand what they are looking for behind this question. A great framework when answering this question is to consider some of the following questions yourself and use those answers in your response:

1. How do other people I have worked with see me?
2. How would other people describe their interactions with me?
3. How would I go about building a team?
4. How have I gotten specific results in the past?

This is an extremely important question to nail because their biggest concern is you being the right fit. If you don't fit them culturally, all of your results and successes will be thrown out the window. Use this question as a way to establish trust create dialogue.

If you have followed the EPIC process getting ready for your interview, you should have a clear understanding of their culture and how you are a great fit.

3. WHAT MOTIVATES YOU?

I talk about it all the time, people make decisions emotionally and they validate those decisions with logic. The question about what motivates you is an opportunity for you to create an emotional connection with the interviewer.

As with the other questions, make sure you keep your response on point and relevant to the opportunity. As you work through preparing your answer, consider the following three questions, both personally and professionally:

1. What do you stand for?
2. What is your purpose?
3. What is your why?

As you formulate the answer to those three questions, think about the relevant examples in your career and how they relate to the opportunity you are vying for in regards to: Impact, growth, technology, teamwork, elevating others, culture building, etc...

4. WHAT ARE YOUR GREATEST STRENGTHS?

This is an opportunity for you to sell yourself by highlighting your unique abilities in relation to the position and role you are competing for. If you have followed the EPIC process, you should be able to effectively align your strengths with their needs.

Somewhere at the towards the beginning of the interview you will have the chance to ask them, "what are the key qualities and traits you are looking for in the person you are considering for this position?" You should already have a fair amount of clarity around this question based on your preparation. However, you will also need to use their answers to this question to know what strengths to focus on.

5. WHAT ARE YOUR SALARY OR COMPENSATION EXPECTATIONS?

It's not uncommon that the interviewer will ask you this question. After all, it is their job to find the best talent at an affordable rate, and it is your job to maximize your value.

Here is the deal, though - you can never answer this question with a simple answer. Giving an answer is lazy and can potentially lower your value. It doesn't matter if your answer is $100,000 or 1,000,000… By giving them an answer, you are telling them that it's really about the paycheck and you meeting your needs. Remember, this can never be about you, it needs to be about them.

That's why it is important to respond with a statement something like, "I really want to learn about the position, what's required, what skill sets you are looking for. I am confident that if I am the right candidate for the job, we can come up with a number that works for both of us. Did you have a range that you were thinking the position was going to earn? That way if it is out of my ballpark, I can save us both time?"

By making that statement, you let them know you are truly looking for the right fit and that it is not all about money. However, you also are bold enough to ask tough questions back and have respect for their process.

However, sometimes they will press you for a range of your own. If that happens, don't evade the question. Give them a big range, and be clear that the range varies based on your responsibilities and performance.

Of all the questions, this is probably the one that makes people the most uncomfortable. It a bit of a cat and mouse game and you need to control the dialogue without seeming like you are trying to evade the question. This is certainly a question you will want to roleplay or record yourself answering until you are comfortable.

6. WHY DO YOU WANT THIS JOB?

When I speak with job seeking executives, I always stress that point that you are not just looking for a job...you are looking for the job. This is your chance to highlight why you are excited for the position.

Once again, while there may be personal reasons like geographic location, short commute, less travel, or other elements that benefit personal and family life, it is best to spend most of your time focusing on the professional aspects of why you want this job. I am not saying you shouldn't discuss the personal reasons, but don't fixate solely on those reasons.

The professional reason you want this job are going to vary widely from executive to executive. I have seen an executive work in a pharmaceutical company for 24 years become bored and feel unchallenged only to become one of the first 1,000 employees of Facebook. Maybe that's you?

What drives you? Do you want to be part of a startup culture or a disruptive technology? Is it important to be part of a company that focuses on sustainability? Are you looking to move from a big public company to a smaller private company because of the impact you believe you can make?

Maybe you were referred into the position from a colleague whom you trust and respect? Either way, be clear on your preparation why you want this job!

Be sure to close your answer with an impact point focusing on your strengths and how they align with the job. It will be different for every position, but once you clearly communicate why you want this job, it is always nice to tie it up with a bow and connect the dots for them on how you are also excited because your strengths seem to be aligned with their needs.

In the sales world, we call this a trial close. If you can get them nodding their head and agreeing with you at the end of every question, it is going to be very hard for them to offer the job to someone else.

7. WHY SHOULD WE HIRE YOU?

This is another tricky question because it is going to depend on your preparation and research. This is a great place to use a story from your past. Hit the emotional connection with them by articulating what experience from your past makes you truly unique and why it matters.

Reflect on what is important to them and use your story to build a bridge that helps to make the picture clear for them. Remember, just because it is clear for you, doesn't mean it is clear for them. It's your job to make it clear.

8. HOW WOULD YOUR CO-WORKERS DESCRIBE YOU?

This is an example of them asking one thing, but meaning another (even if they don't realize it). This is sort of an extension to the question, "what's your management style?" What they are really seeking to find out it, "will you be a good fit for our culture, connect with others, and be easy to work with?"

If you are asked this, be sure to go back to question #2 on this list and use that framework.

9. ANSWERING TWO TYPES OF BEHAVIORAL INTERVIEW QUESTIONS:

Behavioral interview questions will be part of the process with virtually every company. One of the challenges with behavioral interview questions is that it can be difficult to prepare for because they can be very unique. Because of the unique nature of the questions, it is important to have a framework in which you formulate your response.

We recommend using the SOAR framework when formulating your response to any behavioral interview question. SOAR is an acronym for Situation, Obstacle (or Opportunity), Action, & Result. Building your response with this framework will help you create your response in story format, which is concise, memorable and impactful for the interviewer.

A couple examples of behavioral interview questions are listed below.

- **Tell me about a time…?**
    - Example: Describe a difficult work situation or problem and how you had to work within a team to overcome it?
- **How would you handle…?**
    - Example: If one of your co-workers approached you to solicit your support for an initiative that you knew would be great for the company long term, but required you to omit certain information or slightly bend the rules when it came to influencing others within the decision making process, what would you do?
    - Would you call yourself a team player?
    - Have you made any significant mistakes?
    - How did you handle them? What did you learn from them?

Situation:

This is your chance to set the scene. It is the foundation of the story. Explain to them the conditions you faced (think about the environment, your role, deadlines to hit, etc...). Remember, they were not there, so if you jump right into the obstacles or opportunity (which is what many people do) before setting the stage and giving them clarity, your story might not seem relevant to them.

Obstacles / Opportunity:

I say it all the time, companies hire for one reason. They have a problem they need solved. Often times the problem is negative, but it can also be a growth challenge. Regardless, they are looking to bring you on board to solve their problems. Make sure that you spend time during the EPIC prep process to identify any challenges and/or how your going to obtain clarity about the company's problems. Behavioral interview questions will be a fantastic place for you to stand above the competition if you can create a bridge from your past experience and relate it to their current challenges.

Action:

This is your chance to describe exactly what you did to solve the problem. Maybe you had a challenge with a boss or teammate, maybe you had to turn a department around, or maybe it was an internal challenge or one of a plethora of other things. Regardless, here is your chance to highlight how you created your plan of action, and the concrete steps you took to resolve the situation.

Result:

This is your opportunity to bring attention to your quantifiable results. Explain in detail what the results were from your actions. However, as a warning, don't unnecessarily embellish your results as it can backfire very easily. The purpose is to focus on results that prove you brought value to the situation. When you align those desired results with the challenges of the position you are interviewing for, it's a slam dunk.

10. DO YOU HAVE ANY QUESTIONS FOR ME?

So many people make the mistake and don't take advantage of this question. Their response is something like, "not at the moment, I think you covered everything." Think about it this way - they are looking to potentially bring you in as a leader for their organization or department. There is no more certain way to shoot yourself in the foot than not have at least a couple strategic or insightful questions for them.

In fact, even if they don't ask you this question, never leave the interview without fitting in a couple relevant questions in towards the end of the interview. It should not be hard to find the place if you are engaged in an effective dialogue.

Here are some example questions:
- What's the vision for the company?
- How would you describe the company's culture?
- Ask questions relevant to the position the interviewer holds and what's important to them
  - How long have you been working here?

- Ask what is important to them with the future of the company / department / growth
- What risks do you see?
- Where do you see the greatest opportunities?
- How well is the capital funding?
- Is there a big turnover ratio?
- Why did you join the company?
- What do you like most and least about your job?
- Is this a new role or am I replacing someone? Why?
- What is the best person you have ever seen in this role and why?

If you do this effectively, it will be an enjoyable and memorable ending to the interview for all and will set you apart from your competitors vying for the position.

THE LAST THING TO ASK IN THE INTERVIEW

It's vital to handle the conclusion of the interview properly. Before you leave, you should either have a job offer or a time for another interview. Always make sure you get some kind of commitment.

If this is a preliminary, screening interview, your goal is not necessarily to land the job, answer all of their questions or get all of your questions answered. Instead, **your goal is to be invited back.**

> **Therefore, the very last thing you should do is to ask the interviewer, "Where do we go from here? What are the next steps? I am interested and I would like to continue the interviewing process. Are there going to be second interviews? If so, let's get something on the calendar today."**
>
> **If you don't have a commitment by the time you leave that room, there are 25 people coming in right behind you and the interviewers will likely forget you in three minutes. So be sure to schedule a time to come back, or at minimum, a time to call back.**

Don't be afraid to ask questions like, "Who else will I be meeting? Is that person available today? Can I get on that person's calendar?" People don't typically do this because they feel they are being too pushy. However, you are an executive.

You are being hired to be a senior officer in this company. You are there to drive change. If you don't have the ability to get back on their calendar, how the heck are you going to go in and drive change in the company?

> **If you sense that you are being too pushy you can say, "I am sorry if I am pushing too hard, but this is how I get things done. I see clearly what your problems are and I want to come back in a week and lay out the solutions for you. Let's fix this thing. Let's drive change!"**

Remember, you are not interviewing for a job—that's what college graduates do. You are not looking for a job: you are looking for a new challenge. You are looking to drive change. So NEVER go into these interviews and simply answer their questions. Instead, be prepared and confident, make your value proposition clear, propose your 90-day launch plan and get their commitment for the next step—which ideally will be a job offer.

In the next chapter you will learn some vital skills for the job offer and negotiation phase, so you will end up with the position you want at the compensation you desire.

HANDLING THE OFFER AND NEGOTIATION STAGE

If you are handling your search process effectively, oftentimes you will wind up in the offer stage with multiple companies around the same time. You have learned the process of running an effective executive search where you are in control. However, at this stage people often catch a toe and fall flat on their face. They get caught up in the emotion of the offer, or they are uncomfortable negotiating their salary.

Here's the problem: according to statistics quoted in Forbes, by not negotiating, people stand to lose more than $500,000 by the time they reach 60![10]

When you receive an offer, it is the first time a hiring employer is willing to give up the power and let you know that you are the person they want. As a result, they will often put pressure on you to make a decision. Well, you have been handling your entire process proactively to this point, so don't become emotional and reactive now.

---

[10] Jacquelyn Smith, "7 Things You Probably Didn't Know About Your Job Search," Forbes, 17 April 2013, https://www.forbes.com/sites/jacquelynsmith/2013/04/17/7-things-you-probably-didnt-know-about-your-job-search/#4b3767fc3811.

HOW TO RECEIVE AND HANDLE THE OFFER

Typically the initial offer is made by telephone. A person (the interviewer or someone from the HR department) will call you and offer you the position. As we mentioned, this is the first time they are giving up the perception of their control. The way they hold on to some of their control is to put a stipulation on the offer and try to dictate the terms of your response.

Don't bite. Express interest in the opportunity, but tell them you will need 48 to 72 hours to discuss with your husband or wife (or business coach or anyone else you deem appropriate).

That will give you time to review the offer. Be sure to ask them to email you the offer in writing so you can review all the details.

You have remained in control of the process and now have enough time to evaluate the offer, see if it is to your standards and come up with a counteroffer if necessary.

NEGOTIATING THE BEST POSSIBLE OFFER

When you're constructing a counteroffer, the first question you need to ask yourself is "What can I do for them?" John F. Kennedy said it best: "Ask not what your country can do for you, but what you can do for your country." Replace "country" with "company."

Arrange a conference call, and ask for the person to whom you will be reporting to be present. That way you have all decision makers in the room.

Go into the negotiation with a mindset that you don't need the job. Act like you have other offers on the table. (It can be hard to negotiate properly when you have been out of work for six months, but you need to do this if you want to get what you are worth.)

Remember, they are playing on your fear factor with the hope they can get you at a lower price than they are ultimately willing to pay. You need to focus on your value proposition and how it aligns with their needs. If you have handled the EPIC™ Process effectively, this should be very clear to the employer.

Very seldom will a company make their top offer out of the gate, so it is important to understand what to do with that information. There is a wide range of requests you can make during the negotiation to increase your compensation.

1. **Ask for a salary bump.** You know the value you are bringing to the table. Do an assessment of that value in the call and justify your request with clear reasoning.

2. If they hold to the fact that they don't have the budget for a higher salary, ask for a compensation review within 90 days. If you have developed a proper Launch Plan, this should work well.

3. If they are not willing to increase your fixed income, ask for a performance-based bonus.

4. Ask for equity and/or stock options. This can be done in many different ways, but anytime you can negotiate any sort of equity position, it is always advised.

5. Request a signing bonus/moving package. Changing jobs (especially if you are coming from another company) is going to create a lot of extra work for you and your family. Oftentimes there will need to be a signing bonus to compensate for bonuses you are losing from the company you are leaving behind.

Remember, you might not get it all, but if you ask for nothing, you'll get it every time!

HAVING A JOB CUSTOM CREATED

Many top executives have had jobs created for them. The higher you go, the more likely the next position is, if not created just for you, then it will have been reshaped to fit your talents in the course of your discussion with CEOs.

Keep in mind this simple thought: companies hire an executive when they are persuaded that the benefits of having that person on board will sufficiently outweigh the dollar cost. With a "create a job" approach, you can get offers even when no current openings exist. You simply need to present yourself as a solution to a problem.

The most likely companies that may be willing to create an executive job will include organizations that are:
- *growing rapidly*
- *bringing out new products*
- *forming new divisions*
- *acquiring other companies*
- *reorganizing.*

These are the companies that need good people, often from other industries. Plus, they are free to make decisive moves quickly. Entrepreneurs, of course, can create jobs, but so can affluent individuals with large staffs and interests in many organizations.

As you might assume, your goal would be to communicate directly with the person you would most likely work for, or their boss. The key factor to keep in mind is that you will need to be able to communicate a **suitable benefit proposition**. This should be a concise and easily understood description of what you can do. You need to present the promise of tangible value on a scale large enough to warrant an investment in you.

In your initial communication, you need to establish your credentials and mention results achieved in the past. The achievements don't have to be large, but they do have to be significant. Remember, if you have an exciting idea, it may help if you can show how someone else has already used it successfully.

Dealing with opportunities is a key job for many executives. Most don't have enough time and they are predisposed to hear positive news from people who can help them. They will want to believe your message.

You can get your message across by phone or letter. Just make sure your "benefit proposition" is clear and significant.

Identifying the company's needs and vision is very important. Remember, your initial communication held out the promise of a significant benefit. What are your ideas? What makes you confident that they'll work? Do you really understand this company, its problems and its opportunities?

Address these areas, but always remember to convey humility. Acknowledge that the other person has a better grasp of the problems facing the company than you could possibly have.

There are any number of phrases you might use. For example, you might say, "I hope you didn't find my letter too presumptuous. No doubt, you've already given a lot of consideration to these areas." Or, "I don't want to imply that I know your business better than you. However, I do have some ideas that you might not have thought about...." Comments like these set the stage for a cordial exchange of ideas. They can allow you to learn what the employer really wants, build rapport, and focus attention on the areas where you can help.

Your first goal is to find out how the employer views the problem. Ask yourself these questions:

- *What do they see as the key challenges?*
- *What is their "hot button" issue?*
- *Where are their priorities?*
- *What attempts have been made in the past?*

By asking a few questions of the employer and listening carefully, you will find out what he or she really wants. Ask questions and make positive comments in response to the interviewer's remarks. Try to get the employer to share their innermost thoughts—his vision for the firm.

Only when they start to think about this vision and how your achievements might make you a valuable ally in achieving it, will they consider creating a job for you. If you are able to accomplish this in the first interview, that's enough.

In your second interview, you can reinforce your value by drawing a clear picture of the benefits you can bring. Then, build enough enthusiasm to get an offer or be asked to speak with others that need to be involved in the decision.

Keep in mind that your goal is to stir the employer's imagination. The employer should begin to anticipate specific benefits and relate them directly to your talents. Your conversations should focus on the future, with the employer picturing a company already benefiting from your contributions.

Remember, the decision to create a job is as much emotional as it is intellectual, so a dry recitation of proposed improvements won't be enough. You will have to convey enthusiasm and create a sense of excitement.

Be ready to discuss general approaches you would take to reinforce the notion that you will succeed. The best way to do this is to tell stories about your past achievements. If you build sufficient enthusiasm, the employer may conclude the meeting with a statement that they want to create a job for you. Then you can use the negotiation and offer techniques described earlier in this chapter to get the compensation you deserve.

Congratulations on your job offer or creating a job for yourself. **Now go hire yourself a great employer!**

WORK WITH CAREERNEXT

If you have read through to this portion of the book, you have obtained a lot of information that will make your job search far less stressful and much more effective. However, sometimes it can be too much to go about your job search on your own and what you are looking for is a personal advocate.

That is why we created CareerNext. We have created tools, resources, and support that will help virtually every person find their ideal position as quickly as possible. There is nobody in the industry who does what we do. We have some of the best resume writers in the industry, the best online content to help the do-it-yourselfers, and/or have completely customized white glove services and technology to help the busiest executives.

Each day out of work may be costing you $800 a day or more. If you are looking for a consultant and coach to help you avoid the landmines, and get you where you want to go in the shortest time possible, we would love to have a conversation with you.

Visit www.CareerNextAgency.com to learn more.

ACKNOWLEDGMENTS

FROM CHRIS KIRKPATRICK:

Writing this book has been a gift from God. I thank Him for putting all of the people in my life that have helped this come to market and improve lives.

To <u>Matt Baechle</u>, man, I don't know where to start. God has put us in each other's lives for a reason. Thank you for helping take everything I do and help me take it to the next level. We are going to do big things and help a ton of people. The way you saw the vision immediately and jumped in headfirst and committed to everything we are doing is inspiring and humbling.

To <u>Vicki St George</u> of Just Write Editorial & Literary Services, editor extraordinaire: I never thought we would be working together on this project when we met you at Brendon Burchard's event in 2014. Remember meeting Hannah out in the hallway as she couldn't go in with Kanon in tow? (Brendon's youngest fan, at only 6 weeks old! ha! We have the picture to prove it :)

This book would probably have not come together without your help. I had no idea how much work was going to go into creating this. Your support and expertise were beyond expectations and if anyone is ever looking to bring a book to market, they would be lucky to have you by their side. You took what I wrote and made it better than I thought it would be. Your ability to understand this complex, niche market so deeply and so quickly has been very impressive.

To Robert Hotchkin: thank you for the friendship and mentorship. You are not just my pastor—you have become one of my best friends. Thank you for being there for me to call whenever things are not going the way I want them to be that day. Thanks for being you, and being an example of what it is like to be authentic, vulnerable and always striving to be a better person in the eyes of God.

To Clarke Hosp: Thanks for stepping in and helping me FINALLY get this thing done. Your ability to figure things out on the fly is a gift. I am excited for all the projects to come!

To my parents, Bill & Linda, and second parents (in-laws) Reg & Sue: thank you so much for your support (and endless hours of babysitting)! It's funny that when people see this book, they are just going to see the finished work. Only you guys truly know the rollercoaster we have gone through over the past 16 years to get here. (Choking up for a moment….) It's funny how one can work hard for that long and suddenly be seen by the world as an "overnight success." You guys know the truth—the sweat, the dedication, the hours, the tears, the loans, the sacrifices. My gratitude and love for all of you is impossible to express on paper. Just know that I know none of this would have been possible without each and every one of your help at different times in your unique ways over our journey. I hope your three beautiful grandchildren bless you in spades in return.

ABOUT THE AUTHORS

CHRIS KIRKPATRICK  is a former Olympic-level track and field athlete and Top 100 Online Poker Player who took his competitive nature to the business world. A serial entrepreneur, he built his first business at age 22 and expanded it nationally. Since then, he has built teams as Director of Recruiting and Business Development for a Fortune 1000 life insurance company, and oversees a growing private business launch agency.

An expert at recruiting, networking, building teams, and later internet marketing, he fell in love with the executive job search space when he joined an exclusive career management firm to consult on a project. Chris saw the profound positive impact the firm was making in their executive client lives every day and wanted to figure out a way to make the information more accessible to the masses.

He created CareerNext, partnering with his former client Matt Baechle to write this book, and create a suite of digital products that will help more executives advance their careers using time tested and predictable processes and strategies.

Kirkpatrick lives in Chandler Arizona, where he can be found working from his poolside office with his wife and business partner Hannah, playing with his three young children, or off-roading wherever his Wrangler will take him. They enjoy summering in their home state of Vermont to escape the heat.

Kirkpatrick is an extreme entrepreneur, and loves coaching individuals toward their own best life.

MATT BAECHLE is an accomplished Sales & Marketing executive with over 25 years of experience within highly-innovative Medtech and Financial organizations. He's a  creative problem-solver whose held leadership roles within Fortune 500 and start-up disruptive technology companies that have changed lives throughout the world. Matt works extensively with C-suite executives and cross-functional teams to implement programs that change behavior, optimize efficiencies and deliver results.

ABOUT CAREERNEXT

As you have learned by reading this book...

When you are a senior level executive, <u>you can't simply peruse the classifieds for your next career position</u>. Not only are these career positions in high demand, but it is difficult to even get your foot in the door.

CareerNext helps all leaders land their ideal position faster by focusing on a five step process that earns them more income, predictably, with faster results.

That 5 step process is:

Seek Clarity - If you are not clear on who you are, what you do, and more importantly - WHY you do what you do, how can you sell anyone else on that vision? You can't!

Create Your Marketing & Branding Materials - Once you have clarity, you can create all marketing documentation (and social media) to begin your campaign.

Identify & Target - Once you have your marketing & branding set, it is time to identify and target your ideal companies and key decision makers.

Connect & Cultivate - Your ability to land a position in the hidden market will be directly tied to your ability to cultivate and develop relationships with key decision makers and influencers.

Interview, Negotiate, & Close - Navigate every phase of the interview process with confidence. Preparation, interview, plan development, follow up, and negotiation.

CareerNext is dedicated to providing the tools, resources, and support to help you through every phase of your search - **no matter where you currently are.**

LINKEDIN NETWORKING Academy

Industry leading content that will walk you through set up, optimization, and execution on your LinkedIn profile. The course covers everything from the very basic steps of creating your account, to the delicate nuances of how to network with people you don't know online.

LEARN MORE AT CAREERNEXTAGENCY.COM

PERSONAL BRANDING
Academy

Will take you from a blank page to having you positioned as the best investment opportunity in your space. Complete with how to videos, and best practices templates, everything you need to guide you through your resume creation is included.

LEARN MORE AT CAREERNEXTAGENCY.COM

INTERVIEW MASTERCLASS

Navigates you through the complex and uncomfortable interview process. Covering everything from how to prepare for your interview, what to do in the interview, how to create a 90 day plan, how to follow up, and how to negotiate your highest potential financial package. You don't want to go through an interview without this.

LEARN MORE AT CAREERNEXTAGENCY.COM

DONE FOR YOU SERVICES

If you are uncomfortable with the process of creating your own brand online or writing your resume and marketing package, we have a team of experts ready and able to help do it with you. Reach out chris@careernextagency.com for details.

LEARN MORE AT CAREERNEXTAGENCY.COM

Made in the USA
Middletown, DE
28 October 2020